THE WOMAN I AM

My journey from
Richard to Samantha

SAMANTHA PEARSALL

For Richard

TABLE OF CONTENTS

Part One:

LOVING BEGINNINGS

Now if there's a smile on my face
It's only there trying to fool the public
But don't let my glad expression
Give you the wrong impression
Really, I'm sad
Oh, I'm sadder than sad

TEARS OF A CLOWN
SMOKEY ROBINSON AND THE MIRACLES, 1967

1. A HAPPY DEAF BOY

I was born on the 26th of April 1987, a Sunday. My name was Richard and I weighed 8lbs 6zs, the heaviest of all our children. At two weeks old, I was the first baby in the UK to wear hearing aids.

My parents were immensely proud to have three sons; Phillip, the eldest, was born completely deaf. Matthew, the middle boy, can hear. And I was the youngest and also born mostly deaf. More on that later.

I was brought up in the small town of Redcar. It is located near Middlesbrough in the North East of England. The town was made famous by Hollywood producers who filmed "Atonement," starring Keira Knightley and James McAvoy. The film won critical acclaim in 2007, winning an Oscar. One of its most famous scenes was filmed at Redcar Beach, a stone's throw from my parent's home on Kirkleatham Lane.

I grew up in a loving and supportive family. Our home was always cheerful, loud, and busy. There was rarely a dull moment in the Pearsall household.

My parents learned British Sign Language when I was young. Since they now had two deaf children, it enabled them to communicate with us more fluently.

My Mam had her fair share of childhood trauma. She was adopted at age 8. Her mother died in her sleep. She had always been unwell with heart disease. She'd had a coronary artery transplant from a pig which failed and resulted in her death a few days after surgery. My mam visited the hospital and saw her mam sat in an armchair. Her lips were blue, and she looked like a dead body. It frightened her terribly.

One night shortly after the surgery, there was a knock at the door, my mam heard it, and even at that tender age, she knew. It was the police. They'd come to inform us that her mam had died. My Grandad then had to wake my mam that morning to tell her the sad news.

Mam was formally adopted by my Aunt Betty (my grandma's sister) shortly thereafter. Mam was very close to Auntie Betty and Uncle John and saw them as parent figures, she was also close to Auntie Eileen, they were all part of her life and upbringing. My grandad struggled to cope with parenting for a second time. Auntie Betty and her husband, John brought her up in a very loving way. Uncle John was a very tall man! He died suddenly and sadly in London's Victoria railway station after suffering a massive coronary upon leaving the nearby coach station. I think of him every time I am in that station.

The house I grew up in was built by my Mum's dad. It served, at times, as a family hospital. If a family member became ill, they converted the living room into a bedroom. People could die there peacefully, without having to go to hospital.

My family is filled with nurses. My auntie Eileen was a nurse and my dad's mam was also a nurse. There were times having all those medical carers around felt quite spooky, but they don't live there now.

I was a chubby little boy with bright blond hair. We had a big bay window at the front of the house and every morning I would sit there dressed only in a white baby gown and nappy. I waved to my brother as he went off to a special school for the deaf in the minibus.

My hearing brother went to a mainstream school called Scared Heart. At the age of three I was filmed by ITV news, in my home, with my two brothers. I was the first deaf boy to ever attend reception in the mainstream St Dominic's school in Redcar. That was where I first met my schoolteacher, Mrs Lawson. I remembered her being very tall with white hair perfectly coiffed into a large bun. She seemed quite scary to me at that tender age.

Mrs Lawson wanted to collect my coat. I initially and reluctantly answered back "No, I want to keep my coat and my Postman Pat rucksack." I appeared to be in a bit of distress in front of the ITV news cameras. I felt more comfortable having my coat and rucksack on. My Mam was quite embarrassed by my little tantrum and gently reassured me, explaining I needed to take them off, but would get them back later. Eventually I accepted it, and Mrs Lawson hung my belongings on the hook. As I walked into the classroom, I was welcomed by Mrs. Lawson. I remember how nervous I felt being integrated with other hearing children.

Mam got me ready for nursery. She put a big bomber jacket and woolly hat on me, put me in the pram and walked me there. She first dropped my hearing brother off at the school nearby. My dad was mostly in bed after a long night shift at ICI.

ICI is Imperial Chemical Industries, an energy regeneration, plastics recycling, and process research company. Their main site is based in Redcar. He spent 39-years working there and absolutely loved it. He later took voluntary redundancy and despite spending his life working in male dominated industries, cared deeply for me, his transgender daughter, a gay son, and the rest of the family.

When he left ICI, he joined an offshore oil rig in Aberdeen. It was difficult for him because he could not talk about my eventual transition at work, in that heavily male dominated environment, which was understandable.

When I was around 4 years of age, I thought, "why can't I go to the same school as my deaf brother?" I saw him as a role model since we were both deaf. I asked my Mam and she said "yes, that's fine no problem." She applied and I was accepted. Our school was called the Beverley School for the Deaf in Saltersgill, Middlesbrough.

As I grew up, I remembered every day sitting on the sofa next to that big bay window. I had my school uniform on and ate a bowl of cereal, watching cartoon shows. 'Disney's Doug' being my favourite. I looked out of the window waiting for school bus to arrive. Once it arrived, my Mam helped me with my coat, shoes, and bag, before giving me a kiss and waving me and my brother goodbye as we got on the bus.

I have always had a good relationship with the neighbours. I can still remember one neighbour's name, Sylvia. Everyone on the street looked out for each other. Sometimes I'd sit in the bay window with Charlie, people watching. We'd even wave to random strangers periodically. Every Sunday I'd watch out for my paternal grandma who walked to our house. She was always eating an apple.

I remember one day, she walked straight on past the house! I wondered why she was not visiting us today. She soon walked back. She'd knocked on the wrong house door! Her husband died when I was 5. I vaguely remember him but not entirely, I was young.

There was a barbershop and a Chinese takeaway nearby. We were friends with the takeaway owners. They often threw in a box of free noodles with our order! I'm still obsessed with noodles today!

I remember when Matthew went to the barbershop. He was around 12. It was during the time of the David Beckham Mohawk hairstyle. Matthew asked the barber for this cut, but something must have been confusing to the barber. He shaved his whole head!

Matthew rushed home, slammed the door, and ran upstairs crying. He was so very distraught. He explained what happened and my Mam had to try and console him whilst also holding back the giggles! She said maybe he could get some glue and she would stick it back on! That suggestion did not go down well at all. I didn't dare laugh. I had to be careful around my brothers. They were older and much stronger than me. They could easily overpower and beat me up. (And to think, little did they know they were beating up a girl!) It is a memory my Mam still laughs about today.

The Local Authority paid for my bus travel to the deaf school. I remember arriving that first day. There were only five of us in the class, three boys and two girls. In the Beverley school, most of my teachers were qualified up to level 3 in British Sign Language to meet my level of communication. This was my first language and it was nice to be able to communicate with my teachers using my language at such a young age.

They could all sign, even the teaching assistants. Some of the assistants themselves were also deaf which proved to be a positive role model for every deaf child in my school. I also attended Deaf club in the evening as part of socialising.

My deaf identity grew very richly because of such a good level of communication and support both at school and in my home.

2. MAGICAL JOURNEYS

I remember as a family we would travel often by train from Darlington Station to Kings Cross London. The whole family sat at a table on the train eating our homemade packed lunches. As the youngest, I used to sit on either my Mam or Dad's lap. I was quite the clingy and affectionate child.

We regularly visited the Nuffield Hearing and Speech Centre. It was based inside the Royal National Ear Nose and Throat Hospital at Kings Cross.

I remember meeting all the doctors at a very young age. Rather than being frightened, it felt more like the family was going on a holiday. I was too young to understand why we were going there.

I remember the reception area. It had a big playhouse with lots of toys. I loved riding the wooden horse whilst waiting to see the doctor. When our family was called, we went into the room full of light blue MDF (sawdust and glue, fused together under pressure and heat) material. It covered all four walls. It looked as though there were a million tiny holes on the wall as part of the soundproofing.

Again, I sat on my parents' lap, while the doctor checked my ears using the Otoscope (an instrument designed for visual examination of the eardrum and the passage of the outer ear). You have seen them in every doctor's office. When you have cold or flu like symptoms, this instrument has an ear tip, light, and a set of lenses. They also tested my transistor hearing aids, which were popular in the 1980s. I remember it being very heavy and huge! While the doctors talked to my parents about my hearing aids, they would test my level of deafness using an audiometry test machine. This required me to wear a set of headphones and holding a cord with a buzzer to press if I experienced any sound... which I never did. This was a regular appointment, every six months.

The purpose of the continued testing was to see the frequency of sounds I can pick up. My overall level of deafness is severe. The hearing aids amplify sounds and are tailored to the small range of frequencies I can pick up. Thus, the need for regular testing.

I didn't mind it at all. If I'm honest, I kind of liked the attention. I liked the feeling of the ear mould material going into my ear. This was used to make my hearing aids to size. The cool feeling was refreshing. The challenge was to not move my jaw. If I did, it would affect the mould and my hearing aids would whistle.

I tried not to look at my brothers. Their goal was to make me laugh if I looked at them! You must remain very still for a few minutes and that is not easy for a young child.

When in London, we always visited my cousins in Richmond, where they used to live. My mum's cousin now lived in Kent, so we always visited there when I was growing up. They had three children as well and the six of us enjoyed playing outside together. There was a huge willow tree there. I remember it clearly; we always ran down into their garden as if we were running into a large field!! Their garden was massive. My mum's other cousin lived in Richmond, so we used to visit there too.

We would go immediately following my audiology appointments or we would visit for holidays. These trips to London were a part of my childhood. We caught the cross-country train from Kings Cross back to Darlington and would arrive home very late at night!

We lived in a semi-detached house in Kirkleatham Lane near the seaside. As a little boy, it seemed huge. It also had a large back garden.

One summer's day; it was lovely and warm in Redcar. The three of us were playing in the back garden with an oscillating sprinkler. The whole family was outside having a barbecue. At age four, I was the only one running around naked. My brothers wore shorts. I was self-conscious and embarrassed about my body and hid my 'boyhood' between my legs. My brothers were not bothered, but I always felt different.

Indeed, I was not comfortable in my own skin. I felt embarrassed and this was why I 'tucked it away'. My father filmed us all playing in the garden. When we looked back at those old video clips, my family noticed I was hiding my boyhood by tucking them away. As a family, we watched the video and never really thought anything about it.

I always looked at my brothers and felt so different from them. They were very masculine. They could, sometimes, be physical and domineering in how they carried themselves. They were full of bluff, bluster, and fought a lot of the time.

I just did not align with that at all. I was very reserved. While I felt like I should join in fighting with them, I didn't want to. That suppression and self-restraint probably contributed to my rebellious streak. I was a stubborn child. I didn't understand why I felt so differently. It didn't make sense.

I guess at age four I was too young to understand. My boyhood felt alien to me. It started to cause me terrible stress. I did not know what it was. It was like having a wart or something on my body I wanted to get rid of. I couldn't express myself around this. I thought I would just have to live with it. I looked at my brothers who seemed to accept it and thought, why can't I be like them?

3. MY MERMAID

*W*hen I was five years old, my parents took my brothers and me to Toys R Us. They told us we could pick any toy figurine we wanted. My brothers ran straight to the boys' action figure section with 'He-Man' and 'GI Joe.' I headed to the girls' section without even thinking about it. I chose a Little Mermaid doll with red hair. She really grabbed my attention. My brothers chose 'He-Man' toys. My father tried to explain to me that mermaids were for girls. I got cross with him and had a full-on tantrum right there in the store. I didn't understand why he would say that to me at such a young age.

My Mam gently tried to reassure Dad and explained it was only a toy at the end of the day. So, eventually (and because I was spoiled), I got my Little Mermaid doll and took her home with me.

I wanted to take her to school to show my friends, but my Dad stopped me and took it out of my bag. I was furious.

I could not understand why he was so upset and cried about it. My father kept saying I should not do these things. They were 'girl' things. But I challenged him because I was so very stubborn.

It's only now, years later, I know he did it because he cared about me and wanted to protect me from being bullied at school. 1990s societal attitudes were vastly different from today.

I went to school without my mermaid doll and remember a little girl in my class had a 'Beauty and the Beast' doll. I was still terribly angry and upset that I could not take my 'Little Mermaid' doll. So, I just stole her Beauty and the Beast doll to replace my mermaid. I took it home after school and my Mam asked me where it was from? I told her what I had done. She called the girl's Mam and apologised to her. Mam then bought me a Beauty and the Beast doll. I was so happy. I now had both dolls.

Once I snuck my mermaid doll into school. My brother and I got on the school bus. He and his friends sat in the back seat of the bus. They were surprised to see me playing with the doll, brushing its hair. It didn't really bother my brother. He was used to seeing me play with the doll and plait its hair. And I did not think I was doing anything out of the ordinary. My brother's friends asked him, why I was doing it? He could not answer them. He said, "it's just his way."

My girl classmates took in toys I wanted. I neither liked nor wanted to play with what I took into school. I instead wanted to take theirs and play with them, by myself. I was very traumatised by the experience. I could not understand what I did wrong. My brothers could take their toy 'action figures' to school, but I couldn't take mine.

Not just to school either. They could take their toys and play with them in the garden or anywhere for that matter. I did not have the same freedom. My choices were very restricted. I felt very unfairly treated.

I developed a strategy to just accept it. At least I appeared to accept it. I told my dad I wouldn't take the doll to school. And I became particularly good at hiding it in my backpack and sneaking it to school!

I always knew, even as early as ages 6-8, there was something different about me. At age 4 or 5 I just did not understand it. But this incident with my dolls made me realise I was very different from my two brothers.

4. WHAT I REALLY, REALLY WANT

One day I locked myself in the bathroom and wrapped a towel round my body. Not around the waist like a boy does, but higher up round my torso like a woman. I also wrapped a towel around my head (like a woman does) after washing her hair. Nobody was watching, so I felt safe doing this. It was the only time I could feel like a girl. It was an escape. I did not need to apologise to anyone. In that moment, in our bathroom, I knew I wanted to be a girl.

After school, I attended Deaf club sponsored by CDYP, the CHILD Deaf Youth Project. This is a group that provides educational and social activities in a safe environment throughout our local Tees Valley region. Their goal is to help deaf youth gain new skills and challenges to build both confidence and self-esteem.

I tried to fit in with a group of boys, but it never felt the natural thing for me to do. I always gravitated towards and got along well with the girls. And because of this I was picked on every so often.

When my parents went on a weekend away to Scotland or the Lake District, my grandma Mildred would look after us. This was the perfect opportunity for me to experiment. She mostly sat downstairs and watched TV when at our house. I would wander upstairs to my Mam's wardrobe and pick out dresses to wear. I would play with her makeup. I knew Mam would notice that things had been moved, so I always tried to put everything back exactly where it was.

Throughout my school years, I was picked on for being effeminate. I hung out with the girls. I very rarely mixed with boys, that is except my best friend Rusty.

I met Rusty at school. He was in the year behind me. We were like chalk and cheese. We had many similarities. I hung around with girls, so did he. Like me, Rusty is deaf. He had a deaf brother (who was in the year ahead me). I also had an older deaf brother. He had a hearing sister. I had a hearing sibling.

I did not understand what it all meant back then. Maybe my gaydar was developing as I knew there was something that connected and brought us together. When he played, he took his jumper off and tied it around his head like it was long hair. I just knew I could be great friends with him.

I have a good sense of humour and Rusty's is much drier. Yet we get on so very well. Our upbringings were markedly different. Rusty felt I was born with a silver spoon in my mouth! He grew up in a more ordinary council house. His mum was very open-minded. She was great and to this day is my second mum. His household used lots of colourful language. This was quite different to what I was used to at home. It all really made me laugh. I also felt I had neutral space to talk. I was more accepting of what his Mum had to say.

They say mothers and/or parents know best. I knew they were usually right in the end but because they were my parents, I often didn't want to hear what they had to say. Rusty's mum passed her personality traits on to him. He is completely non-judgmental and can remain neutral. But he will always say what he thinks, regardless of what other people think. In the North East of England, that was a rare trait!

I'm more of a pushover. I give in too easily. Rusty though, is stubborn and always true to his word. I am always protected by him from being hurt. He always looks out for me. When we are out socialising at Deaf events, he is a good judge of character and honestly knows whether a man is right for me or not.

Rusty and I were always good friends in school and became intimately closer when we left school. I think I broke his heart though when I came out as transgender and ended that part of our relationship. I think I came out quicker in some ways because I needed to show him, I wasn't ending it for the sake of hurting him. I needed to be my true self.

Rusty had a thing for small men which is what I was back then. But now as a woman, he's like 'no thank you!' And that's probably why we can be best friends.

In his eyes, I am irreplaceable. He appreciates my laid-back nature. I don't take things to heart. I laugh at things I shouldn't laugh at and he's completely on the same wavelength. All we need to do is give each other 'a look' and we know instantly what the other is thinking. He got me into trouble quite easily by being so mischievous. He has a big personality, and most can't help but like him.

It made me very defensive when anyone called me out for hanging out with the girls. I had to deny it because I knew I would be bullied at school.

When there were special events in school such as Red Nose Day or other charity fund raisers, they were often fancy dress. I would use these opportunities to dress up as a girl and thereby fulfilled my dreams of being one. I knew I could not always do this. My brothers already teased me for being too 'girly.' So, I would quickly cover up that fact and try not to pick girly things for EVERY event, even though I would have loved to.

I was very anxious about it in those early days. Rusty and me always dressed up for Red nose day.

Constant stress caused anxieties. When I was around 16-18, after having left school, I stayed over at Rusty's house most of the time. It was an escape from my brothers and their constant fighting.

I fought more with Phillip. We were both Deaf and had the same circle of friends. The Deaf community is very small, so this is common. Phillip knew exactly what to say (sign) to push my buttons and wind me up. And the same is true in reverse. Matthew was not Deaf, so I think he was slightly removed from us in that perspective.

At home I had to defend myself against them. Although outwardly it might have appeared a fair fight since we all looked similar, inside I was weak and fragile and did not want conflict. It really wasn't anyone's fault. Nobody knew how I felt. Rusty's mum used to buy my favourite dish, chicken parmo, every time I stayed there! It's a dish found only in the North East; you cannot get it around the country. It is battered deep fried chicken with melted cheese. It was delicious! All 3000+ calories of it! This is when things started to shift with Rusty from friends to a little bit more.

I used to pinch Phillip's clothes because he had such good fashion sense and bought expensive clothes. If I ever had to style myself, I would not know what to wear! He would come home, and I would be dressed in his clothes. He would say, "who gave you permission to wear my clothes?" And much to his frustration I would reply saying, "I don't need to ask!"

I tried to fit in that way. I didn't bother stealing Matthew's clothes because, being a straight person, he was clueless with what to wear. I was not at all keen with his fashion sense! Also, I would not have dared to take Matthew's clothes. He was much scarier and tougher than Phillip and would have targeted me even more. He was strong. I learned the hard way by being on the receiving end of his fists!

During most weekends, I normally spent time in my bedroom. My hearing brother got really annoyed with me. I loved listening to music and watching music videos. I would play it very loudly. Yes, you read that right. I loved listening to music, and I am deaf.

My level of Deafness is quite severe. I cannot pick out high frequencies like a smoke detector or fire alarm. But low bass frequencies I can hear. The music I listen to is low and has a strong pop/house beat to it.

Cheesy pop music is very catchy and repetitive. So, I would practice listening to the music, and reading the lyrics at the same time. Sometimes my mam would guide me with sign language and say, "it's started." Eventually I learned the music lyrics by heart and with the right timings!

All of this was possible, of course, only with my hearing aids. Without them I cannot hear any music unless it's on full blast. In this situation I could hear the beat and the rhythm, but not the lyrics. Without hearing aids, I cannot hear much but I can hear loud, low frequency noises such as banging. I have a better level of hearing compared to my brother who is profoundly deaf.

My parents had a record player. My dad loved the Jackson 5. I still love the 'Don't blame it on the boogie' track and Michael Jackson's 'Billie Jean.' I used to use his big headphones which went over my ears and hearing aids, listening to this track. I would fall asleep to it. Mam and dad would turn it off and carry me up to bed.

Music is a cure for my stress. It wiped out all the struggles I faced in the world. I use music as a therapeutic practice. Some of the songs I listen to, make me cry. I have such a strong emotional attachment to them. They bring back memories of the pain I was going through back then.

If I experience trauma now, am bitter about something, or heartbroken, I listen to music. Rusty knows me so well. He is like 'oh here we go!' Every time the music is cranked up full, he doesn't need to ask; he just knows something is up.

When I was younger, I locked myself in my room and played cheesy pop music: Britney Spears, Spice Girls, B*Witched and Take That. I always had music blaring away. My brother Mathew would storm into my room in a foul mood and tell me to turn it off! He would also have a go at me, saying how 'gay' I was! It was always my hearing brother since my deaf one, Phillip, could not hear it at all, so the sound level did not bother him.

Matthew was usually cross when his hearing friend was around, and my pop music played loudly in my bedroom. Having different musical tastes, my pop music really embarrassed my hearing brother.

I was a big fan of the Spice Girls. My parents took me to a concert in Manchester and that remains the best childhood memory.

Even today, I remain a huge Spice Girls fan. Older people love Abba. But the Spice Girls were huge to my generation and I still adore them so very much!

Even now, listening to this music brings back so many happy childhood memories of when I would sing with my mam while she was busy in the kitchen. As soon as the Spice Girls appeared on MTV, I'd shout across the room to let her know. She would run into living room from the kitchen and sing along with me using British Sign Language.

When my mam joined in sign singing, it brought me even closer to the music. You can really sense the emotion through the beautiful language in our hands. It bonded us together as well as me to the music. If she was not there, I didn't feel that same connection. My feelings weren't quite as strong. Watching my mam signing always brought a smile to my face. It's like I can finally get access to the information I need.

When my dad went to America for a work project, he asked what present I would like him to bring back? I said, "a Britney Spears album and a Mickey Mouse teddy bear." He got both for me and I was over the moon with my new album. My two brothers were not impressed. I did not care!

5. FOOTBALL AND EATING

W hen I started secondary school at the Beverley School for the Deaf, I was frightened seeing all the Sixth Form boys and girls. I was 5-6 years younger than most of them and anxious. I was so small in stature compared to them.

I went to a deaf school, but they could not provide certain parts of the curriculum needed for me to take the GCSE exams. My parents wanted me to have those exams, so a few of us went to the mainstream school next door. It was a much larger school called the Newlands School. It was also a Catholic school. I went there to continue with the GCSE curriculum and take the exams.

I was very anxious at Newlands School. There were so many boys and girls compared to the deaf school, where the classes were much smaller. While at Newlands, I learned to stuff my feelings down to fit in more with the other students to prevent bullying.

Unfortunately, as I suppressed my feelings, this led me to start over-eating. I was not happy with myself. At around 10-12 years of ae, I became obese. Because of this, I was also bullied.

I decided to join the football team to cope with my feelings. The football team was called the Eston Middlesbrough Football Academy. Affiliated with the perennial heart-breaking team that yo-yoed its way up and down the Premier League tables to the Champions and at times Division

One. We were coached by Frank Spraggon and George Cochrane, both former professional footballers. They became my mentors.

As the only deaf child on the team, I naturally received more attention than the others. I enjoyed playing football. They made me feel included and it helped relieve my internal stress and turmoil. I did not really want to play football. But I began to enjoy it because it made me look 'boyish.' It helped me cope with my identity stress, but in hindsight, it was truly horrible.

Unfortunately, Beverley School for the Deaf closed because the Local Authority could not provide enough funding. All deaf pupils were mainstreamed. I had no option but to go to the Coulby Newham school. It had a PHU (partially hearing unit), which was a mixture of deaf, hard of hearing and hearing pupils. I was educated in both settings.

I carried on preparing for my GCSEs there. And I also carried on covering up my effeminate ways and trying to blend in. The older I got, the better I was able to hide my true feelings. I became very skilled at it.

I constantly ate and stuffed my face because it made me feel better. Eating seemed a comfort, but outwardly it had the opposite effect. I gorged on junk food like pot noodles, pizza, crisps, bars of chocolate and drank litres of cherry coke. There was a petrol station a short walk from my parents' house. I would go to there to the shop and buy enormous amounts of junk food. The kilos climbed for years into obesity. I developed moobs – 'man boobs.' I was mortified and embarrassed.

I was so confused with my identity, I wanted to keep my breasts, but mentally it was not a right fit for then. I remember talking to my mam and dad about having moobs, and my mam said, "it was normal." I was thinking, want neither boyhood nor moobs, it needs to be one or the other!

I felt like I was wrestling with my body, I was tormented. It was difficult to process it all. My moobs ultimately triggered my eating disorder.

So, playing football was an attempt to transform my body. I wanted to get rid of my moobs. I could not cope with them. I hated my boyhood but as I had all my life and learned to manage it. With the moobs, although it was what I wanted, it would have meant coming out then. I was not ready for that.

Playing football worked. I cut out the junk food. I knew eating crap food was affecting my moobs. Within about 6 months, I noticed a change. I was losing weight and felt I looked better. I was able to get the same comfort from looking slimmer that I did from eating junk food.

A relative of my deaf brother's girlfriend worked in a butcher's shop. He would bring my mam a big box of meat, which she bought from him regularly. My diet became steak, vegetables, and boiled potatoes. I ate this for a long time and started to lose weight. This became the only thing II would eat and I eventually lost a lot of it. I was also playing a lot of football at the time, so I became healthier and fitter. I told people I was losing weight because of all the football I played. But by now I realised I had an eating disorder. I used football and eating meat and vegetables as an excuse to cover up all my unresolved internal issues.

It became obsessive with me and I fixated on eating the same meal. For some reason, I ate steak, vegetables and boiled potatoes and I would not deviate from this. I was becoming a problem child and caused my parents stress.

They tried to encourage me to eat something else, but I dug in my heels in and would not. I remembered on a family holiday to Disney World in Orlando. It was an amazing holiday, but I spoiled it. Steak was not always on the menu so my parents ordered a KFC bucket, but I wouldn't eat it. I said, "no, it's too fatty!" If I couldn't have steak, I would just eat a salad.

Anything oily or fatty remains a trigger for me today. When Rusty makes a fried egg, I shout, "what are you doing, you don't need oil?!"

He says, "relax!"

I say, "but it's a non-stick pan."

And he finally says, "do it yourself then!"

Fried foods trigger me. I really struggle to deal with it. Living together, we argue about the choice of food in the house. When we shop, he will pick fatty foods or chocolate. I struggle because I know I'll end up eating it.

When we order takeaways, we bicker because I will say, "can we split it and just have half each?" He says, "no I want a full meal, you order your own" and I say, "fine we won't have a takeaway then!" So, he gives in and it makes me feel better that I have some control over my caloric intake. I know it is all a long-term consequence of my earlier experiences.

At age 15, I had to stop playing football due to the club's age limit. I reverted to overeating again because I was unhappy. It was a constant battle, a cycle that just repeated itself.

I always had issues with my weight. I only realised, working in mental health services the last few years, I have an eating disorder. I grew up in a society where women must look perfect. Reading magazines, watching television adverts, and looking at photos of someone else's idealisation of perfection. I now know that they are all airbrushed and highly unrealistic, but because I have known that influence for so long, it made me very body conscious. I still feel that way now.

I feel airbrushing of models should be banned. We should be teaching young people about their humanity rather than striving for unachievable and unsustainable images.

When I came out as trans in 2010, I was a little overweight. But I was happy. My overeating stopped, and I began to lose weight. I immediately developed an eating disorder again, this time in the other direction. I felt pressure from society to look perfect. Now I restricted myself to less than 500 calories per day. I was eating homemade soup (so I could monitor exactly what went into it), with one slice of toast, without butter, and drank a cordial with water and diet coke. Sometimes I would treat myself to 30 grams of cereal. I'd eat it dry or with a small amount of milk. I weighed and tracked every morsel that passed through my lips.

At work in the mental health hospital, they had a kitchen. The staff would order their dinners in the morning to prepare for our break. On occasion I forgot to order my meal, but chef knew I would have salad and she prepared it for me anyways. She knew I would always have ham, tuna, or chicken salad, depending on what was available. I began smoking cigarettes to suppress my hunger. I was up to 20 silk cuts per day.

This continued for years and I became painfully thin. I was a size 0 (UK size 4). In male clothes that meant I went from a waist size of 34 to 26 AND still needed a belt! I lost 5 dress sizes in female clothing, from size 14 to size 4. I now fit into children's age 12 clothing. The disorder contributed to my hair loss, my breath smelled awful, my skin and scalp were bone dry. I was physically lethargic and felt terribly ill.

Mentally, I felt great. I felt I looked good, but my body wasn't in a healthy place at all. My parents couldn't monitor me because I was living in Manchester. They were horrified when they saw me, and said it was not attractive. My line manager at work also saw something was wrong. She said I was too thin. I spoke up and came out to her before I came out to my parents. I was in a dark place for a long time living with this.

When I moved to the Isle of Wight in 2012, I began to eat again. I was in relationship, I was happy. I was a deputy manager of a care home and of course old people love to eat traditional meals. The chef at the care home would make my favourites such as cottage pie, steak pie and mash and more. It was all so delicious, I couldn't refuse. She fed me very well.

She knew how much I loved her food and so when I worked the night shift, she left me a plate wrapped in clingfilm, with a note 'especially for you', as well as a pudding of sponge cake with jam and coconut on top with custard.

But long before that period of relative happiness, I had so much buried under the surface that just bubbled and boiled. I was not addressing my gender identity issues. I began mixing with the wrong people at Coulby Newham and so to fit in, I covered up who I really was. I outwardly became terribly angry, cocky, and feisty.

I drank Lambrini in the streets after school. My parents were completely unaware. I ate a ton of chips and smoked. I funded it all by working in a Pizza Shop in Redcar. My friend's father owned the shop. It was just the beginning of a massive change in my teenaged life.

As I moved schools, I found a group I could hang around with thinking if I were able to fit in, I wouldn't be bullied. I just hoped my identity issues would go away. This group was the type to get into fights. While I didn't join in, I observed and learned what they did and how they did it.

I used this to my advantage and from 16-18 this is when the all-out wars began with my brothers. For the first time, I could seriously challenge them both and was a real threat. It was mainly with Phillip. I had so much anger inside of me. I more mouthed off to Matthew, I tried to be clever and wind him up. He did not like it at all. With Phillip, I fought more. I discovered I had more strength than I realised. We would physically beat the crap out of each other. We would throw things and hit each other with objects. It caused my parents a lot of stress.

Matthew dated a Deaf girl called Katie. She was blonde and thin, but she would get in the middle of our fights and try to stop us from hitting each other. She stuck around and they have been together ever since, now happily married with 2 children. So, a result of the fighting was my two beautiful nephews.

One Friday night a group of us, mainly boys and some girls, drank and smoked in a pedestrian tunnel. The others had an advantage over me. They could hear and started running. It wasn't until I saw blue lights flashing, that I realised it was the police! I panicked. We all ran away from the approaching police car to the other end, knowing it wouldn't to fit through the tunnel.

Of course, they knew our strategy and four of them stood there like a shield blocking our escape. I tried to run, but they grabbed me! I thought I have been caught by the police! They told us that we shouldn't be drinking, poured away our alcohol and asked where we lived. I lied and said, 'over there.' They said, "OK, so what's your address?" I didn't know an address in the area, so I had to give my real address. They made a list of all our names and addresses. This was not in my nature at all. I literally crapped my pants. I was physically shaking. I was the angel compared to my brothers. I knew my parents would kill me if they found out. That was the warning and wakeup call I needed to stay away from that wrong crowd.

I got the last bus home and hoped my mam and dad would be in bed, not able to smell smoke which I tried to cover up with chewing gum! I crept upstairs praying they wouldn't catch me. I waited for them to say something the next day, but they never did. I'd gotten away with it.

To this day they don't know about it and will find out when they read the book. But I honestly think nothing about me shocks them anymore!

6. DEEPENING SPIRAL DOWNWARD

hen I left Coulby Newham, I went to the Cleveland College of Art and Design in Middlesbrough to study fashion. I was interested in fashion because of my aunt's brother, Peter Fionda. He was a fashion designer in London and had attended this college. So, it was the obvious choice.

During college, I was always out socialising and rarely home. My parents started to question why I was not home much. My time was spent either at deaf club, a social gathering, or I would stay at a friend's house. I was between the ages of 16-18 while attending that school. I worked handing out leaflets for the Pacific pub, which my friend's father owned. I had a scooter for a short period and would ride into town. I also visited friend's houses for takeaway or chicken curry. This resulted in us staying up late into the night laughing the time away. Indeed, we lost all track of time, which often was often around 3:00 am.

I needed to escape my brothers who were older than me and always arguing and fighting. This caused my parents a lot of undue stress. My deaf brother and I had the same circle of friends. He never told me what he was doing and when I turned up somewhere, he was already there!

The family home was happy until I left school at age 16. The years between 16 and18 changed dramatically as I grew more and more unhappy. It felt the best thing for me was to be out of the house as much as possible. If I was away from my brothers, we avoided confrontation. They would pinch my clothes, wind me up, and display behaviour problems that further incited my anger.

My older brother came out as gay (when I was about 17). This piled extra pressure on me. I could not come out and worried for my parents and how they would cope if I came out as transgender. So, I kept it all to myself.

At 18, I left home and lived in a flat with two other boys...near Stewart Park in Middlesbrough. Finally, I could do as I pleased without answering to anyone.

While I'd left home, I still had to pretend and 'play the game' because I was living with two boys. The reason I continued to pretend was because the area was very poor and a rough place to live. There was zero tolerance of LGBT people in any way, shape, or form. It was anything but a multi-cultural society. There was almost no diversity and the residents were all very closed-minded.

Things might change for me, I thought, if I tried to meet a girl. That turned out to be my biggest mistake ever. It was brutal for me. Just awful. I was not at all proud of myself. I tried to be macho and it felt all wrong because I had serious gender issues.

Inside I felt like a girl. Here I was trying to meet another girl! This all felt very wrong. I tried to use her to cover my real feelings and carry on the pretence. It was a complete non-starter of a relationship.

I met her through Rusty's brother, they were friends. She was hearing and lived a 10-minute walk from my flat. She liked me. I thought, 'Jesus Christ, I cannot cope with this. I don't want this,' I thought, but felt I had something to prove I'm straight.

It made me feel ill. It got to the point of intimacy, but I thought, 'oh my God, this is not for me.' I felt like I was going to throw up. And it was no fault of hers. She was nice, but I had no attachment to being with her. I felt like I was having sex with someone of the same sex as me. It felt wrong. It was awkward. It was not in any way pleasurable and still gives me the creeps just thinking about it.

I think she liked me a lot, but I didn't feel the same way in return. I was most worried my friends would wonder if I was gay if I didn't pursue her. This was to be my 'proof' I wasn't gay. Which is a horrible place to be.

It happened one night. I explored it, but it wasn't for me. That was the first and last time with her or any girl for that matter. Rusty had already come out as gay and said he would not touch a girl with a bargepole and never has. It was all more difficult for me knowing deep inside I was trans.

After Fashion school, I attended St Martin's College in Middlesbrough. It was right behind my old flat at Stewart Park. I studied accountancy, bookkeeping, and business. However, now age 18, my attendance dropped off and my life was in a big slide. I was skipping college. The motivation to learn was gone. Somehow my parents found out about my poor attendance at college.

My mam texted me to see how I was because I was living away from home. She asked if I was in college, I said no because I was not well. Sometimes she'd text and asked if I had been to college. I'd wait until after 5 pm to reply I had been.

As the slide continued, I got into arrears with my flat rental payments. The landlord contacted my mam. I was busy clubbing, partying, and spending money on clothes. I also applied for a credit card, but they didn't know about it. It didn't feel good to lie, it's not in my nature to be dishonest. They brought me up well and made sure I had access to a good education, but I was throwing everything away. My priorities were all wrong.

Mam knew something was wrong and forced me to come back home. I moved back when I was 19. When I moved back, mam or dad would drop me off at college to ensure my attendance. I managed to catch up on everything I missed and got my qualifications in the end. Those qualifications made me feel immensely proud.

When I finished college, I became further unwell emotionally. My parents could see my mood changing for the worst. I had always been a happy, lively boy. Now I was not myself. That bubbly personality was gone.

I was always going out at night. I gambled, constantly drank, and played snooker at a late bar called Riley's. It was usually open 24-hours a day. I would stay there all-night playing while my family slept. Rusty's Mam always came and collected us as soon as we walked out of Riley's, usually at 5am. Rusty's Mam waited outside in the car, in her dressing gown, with her hair tied up in a ponytail. She saw us and gave a disapproving look and signed to us through the window. "Eeeeee, what time do you call this?!" And then jokingly said, "Get in the car."

Just before I turned 20, I gave up my flat in Stewart Park and moved back home with Mam and Dad. I went through a period of deepening depression. I was struggling with my identity. Mam said she remembered looking out the kitchen window while washing up and saw me sitting in the garden on the swing. I was still in my dressing gown, smoking heavily, my hair looked thin and my Mam knew I was becoming very ill.

Something needed to be done.

7. DEAF AND TRANS

I remember locking myself in the bathroom again and wearing bath towels like I did as a young child. Going through puberty was torture. I was now growing facial hair, my manhood sickened me, and everything felt disgusting.

The bathroom was the only place I could feel like a woman. I was now in my early 20s and grew more and more frustrated. I was covering up too much of me which was why my depression became so severe.

I knew I was in the wrong body.

When in the shower, I thought to myself, "what can I do? I had a fantastic childhood, was well cared for, and my parents didn't know what triggered my misery.

In the shower, I sat squarely on the horns of a dilemma. I really wanted to change my gender but could not. In that moment I felt there was no help for me.

Being deaf meant also living in a silent world where I already missed out having lots of information. I rely heavily on my eyesight, not being able to hear. I never heard or picked up anyone talking about transgender, gender reassignment, transition, or any of those things at a young age. I was also unable to hear what was said on the radio. I feel I suffered from language deprivation as I missed out on a lot of information that hearing people would have easily had access to. My family was able to communicate with me, but my family wasn't the issue - the issue was with society. Without my family I would have missed out on a whole lot more!

So, I missed out on lots of information during childhood because I could not hear things around me in everyday life. I felt like I was the odd one out, the only person in the entire Deaf community who dealt with being deaf and transgender. I didn't know how or who I could turn to for advice and support.

I came out as gay at 20, only because I knew there were a few deaf gay communities I could join. But I told my family I was bisexual. I wanted to break the news to them gently. So, I went out to gay bars and felt slightly happier. I was able to meet gay men. Even though I knew it wasn't for me, it was the only option I had for now.

This is why my passion for transgender education in the deaf community is so strong. I want young people to be free to learn and begin having conversations about gender at a much earlier age.

Part Two

JOURNEY TO TRANSITION

Well, I've been 'fraid of changin'
'Cause I've built my life around you
But time makes you bolder
Even children get older
And I'm gettin' older, too
I'm gettin' older, too
Ah, take my love, take it down
Oh, climb a mountain and turn around
And if you see my reflection in the snow-covered hills
Well, the landslide will bring it down

LANDSLIDE

STEVIE NICKS, FLEETWOOD MAC, 1975

8. ALL TUMBLES DOWN

One day I was sitting in our living room. I had been neglecting myself, not dressing or eating, and chain smoking. My father knew something was wrong. I sat with my head in my hands and said, "I just can't cope anymore." Dad knelt beside me and asked, "what was the matter?" I burst into tears, my emotions flowing all over the place. I thought, "I can't tell my father the truth." So, I blamed it on debts, bills, and credit cards. I sat there blaming everything else but... myself.

Dad said he would pay off the debt for me since he could see I was so ill. The debt was from gambling, smoking, and buying clothes. I wanted to look and feel good. This seemed the only way I could feel better. For me, spending money was a coping strategy. It was a way to make me feel comfortable because I felt so guilty knowing I could not be the person I really wanted to be.

Dad paid off all my debt and I was incredibly grateful. Some of the pressure was lifted. But I didn't think I was capable of working. I was just not well inside myself. It was a wonderful gift and a massive help that Dad did this for me.

When I came out as gay... not trans. I needed to break it to my parents gently, one step at a time, especially since they already had one gay son.

When I came out as gay, I explored and started to see gay men... or at least I tried. I just did not find them appealing in the slightest. However, when I was in gay bars, I always fancied straight men. I found them attractive. But I knew it would never work. When I figured out why, it just was more infuriating.

9. MANCHESTER, IT ALL COMES FROM HERE

I turned 21 in 2008 and moved to Chester Road in Manchester, near Old Trafford Stadium. It still holds a special place in my heart. I got my first job working at St Mary's Hospital in Warrington as a Rehabilitation Co-Therapist in the deaf forensic unit. This was my first role in a mental health setting.

Manchester is a vibrant, multi-cultural city and it really opened my eyes to life. I used to go to Canal Street, the gay village, with a group of friends. I loved partying every weekend there and it was one of the first times I dressed up as a drag queen. This was to display what I felt was my 'true' identity. It was the only way I could cope with my 'hidden' identity plus it made me feel a lot more feminine.

For nearly three years without fail I would go out every weekend dressed and made up as a drag queen. Over this period, I saw gradual changes in my appearance as a drag queen. I was becoming more of a transvestite as opposed to a drag queen. It was a slow transition to a more formal version of being a transvestite.

My clothing and make up became more precise and more feminine as opposed to the over-the-top clothing and painted on drag makeup. I took great pride in my appearance as a female, looking after my skin, hair, and everything about the way I looked. My style of clothing became important because I had to blend in.

I also realised for the first time in my life I was so happy to be able to dress up as a member of the opposite sex. I felt content and normal. I noticed a pattern where I always felt down every time I reverted to my original gender, removed my make-up, wigs, and dress. This was when my depression returned. I could never be happy with my true self.

I also noticed that straight men were starting to find me attractive as a transvestite. This spurred me on in my cause to become transgender and I finally found my identity. I had been searching for this my entire life without knowing what it was.

I was apprehensive though since straight men did not know my true identity. I suffered with the anxiety not knowing whether or not to tell them. Early on, I decided to always tell them the truth. Otherwise I knew there could be dangerous consequences. I needed to protect myself from being both physically and emotionally hurt. Someone like me was unusual in society at that time.

Surprisingly, things went fine, and most men accepted me without question. They did not see me as being different. And as a result, I became more assertive and self-confident.

I have always been overly cautious because I know being deaf and transgender made me feel naturally vulnerable. I always thought I might face dual discrimination.

I was very self-conscious about my weight at this time and that re-started my eating disorder. It made me realise I had to something about it. Whilst working in the forensic unit at St Mary's hospital, I was struggling with my identity. I also saw how some of the patients were affected, the struggles they went through. It made me begin to focus on myself.

I remember working the night shift and doing hourly patient observations. Normally you observe them through slatted window blinds. I would see a patient on the bed, very unhappy and looking depressed. I thought, that could be me if I did not sort myself out.

During a supervision session at work, my manager raised concerns about my weight. She saw changes in me and knew something was not right. Her concern was the same as my family and friends. I was battling with an eating disorder and would never admit it to my family, colleagues, or friends.

During another supervision session I decided to be more open with my manager. I told her I wanted to change my gender and transition from male to female. She was, naturally, quite taken aback. But because I had been so open and honest with her, she initially advised me to speak to my family, which I was very reluctant to do. But one summer's day I decided to visit my family in my hometown.

Unfortunately, when I tried to break the news gently about my gender issues, my cousins were also visiting. It was not the right time to 'come out' to my family as I felt too much pressure. The next day I still could not go ahead with it and was back at square one. My Mam knew something was not quite right. Before my parents left to go to their caravan for the weekend, Mam said my voice sounded different, more emotional. I just covered it up and said I was fine.

My Mam also noticed my appearance had changed. I was quieter than normal, and she saw my weight loss. I went back to Manchester as there was nothing for me in my hometown. On the train back I was overcome with a flood of tears and felt very stupid. I texted my parents when I arrived. It felt cowardly but was the best and easiest way out for me.

My text read something like: "I don't want to hurt anyone in the family, but I couldn't 'come out' on Friday as my cousins were there at the house. I just want to explain I think texting you is the best way for me to let you know that I want to change from being a male to female. I have had gender issues for a long time. I hope you can both support me, but if not I'm happy to do it alone."

I had to be strong to prepare myself for rejection.

Both of my friends were home in the flat and saw me sitting on my sofa in a flood of tears. They asked me what was wrong? I told them the truth. One friend's face was visibly shocked. Despite being gay, it was hard for him to accept this. I think at some level, he was fearful of losing his friend "Richard." My other friend, a female, accepted it much better. She reassured and hugged me saying everything was fine.

When my parents received my text, they were in their static caravan in the village of Swainby. When I texted to tell them, I was going to transition, they fell to their knees and sobbed, absolutely heartbroken. Coincidentally, earlier that same day, my Dad learned his employment was coming to an end. After 39-years of service, he took voluntary redundancy.

Had I known this, I would never have come out to them then and there. I never wanted to upset my parents, but the whole process could have faced even more delay. That could have done more damage than good. So, maybe it was a blessing.

They decided to go home. Phillip was there with his partner at the time, Laurent. My mam and dad told Phillip and Laurent what happened. Naturally, Phillip was extremely supportive of my parents. As a family they decided to drive to Manchester right then to support me.

Phillip and Laurent stayed with friends in central Manchester. I did not realise until quite recently, that mam and dad thought I was going to commit suicide when they received my text.

To be fair, they were right to think that. I was in such a bad place, anxious and nervous, waiting for their arrival. I sat chain-smoking on the stoop, fag after fag. I must have gone through a pack of 20 in less than an hour!

I was terrified of what was going to happen. I thought they might shout at me and disapprove. Perhaps even try to forbid me from having the surgery. My thoughts were running wild, 'what would they say, how would they react?' I knew deep down they would never yell at me. But I could not help thinking this way. I was not in a right frame of mind. I could only think the worst. No positive scenarios played out in my mind.

I remember when they arrived. I was completely panicked, so very scared. I wished I had not said anything and wanted to go back in time... to not tell them or say anything. I saw sadness, upset, and heaviness in their eyes. This was something I hated to see.

They walked me into the flat, straight to my bedroom. They wanted privacy because Rusty and Sureen were in the living room. I remember it all so vividly. I had my arm up, covering my face. I was crying my eyes out; I was just so distraught and could not bring myself to make eye contact. That would mean having to communicate. Hearing people can communicate without looking, Deaf people cannot!

It is even more difficult. Mam and dad were trying to get me to look at them. Mam sat on the side of the bed, rubbing my arm to try and get my attention. I was hurting and saw their hurt. I was the cause of it all.

Everything building up to this point finally came to a head. I was so scared about what the future held. I did not know how things would work out. My emotions were all over the place, I could not think straight.

My parents were shocked and did not take it all on board straight away. They were practical with their help rather than emotional and probably just thought it was a phase I was going through in my life. They felt living in the big city was affecting me.

Mam and Dad talked to me and together we decided the best thing was to see a specialist. Mam helped me complete the application form. I did not know what to say and it was quite remarkable she supported me. We sent it off to the gender identity clinic along with a referral from my GP.

I had to wait nearly four months before being seen by a psychologist at the Gender Dysphoria Clinic at Central Manchester University Hospital. This clinic aims to both treat and support people with gender dysphoria and help them to live their life the way they prefer. In their preferred gender identity. The only clinical procedure done that day in Manchester was a blood test and to this day I still do not know why!

The waiting was torturous. I was neither well nor of sound mind. Every day felt like forever. The long wait to be seen by the doctor for my assessment was very depressing. I thought, 'you must be kidding me. This is taking far too long. I cannot go on like this.' Every day that passed was about survival. A means to get a day closer to the assessment. Even though I thought, every day was a day closer, it did not make it any easier. It was taking forever. There was no joy or pleasure during those days. It was just a waiting game.

The amount of time was ridiculous. No wonder there is such a high rate of suicides in the trans community. If someone had a mental health crisis, they could go to A&E and receive an immediate assessment. Waiting 18-months for an 'initial' assessment felt, frankly, like the system 'taking the mick' out of me, 'pranking me.'

There should be a process for trans people, already marginalised by society, to be seen straight away. And not having to wait so much longer than others for their next appointment. At least they then would feel acknowledged and know they have something to work towards and look forward to... a light at the end of a very dark tunnel.

When I had my first assessment appointment to see if I were a suitable candidate to undergo further treatment, we agreed I would need a referral to the Gender Identity Clinic (GIC) in Hammersmith, London.

10. CH–CH–CH–CH–CHANGES

*B*efore my first appointment, I reinforced with the doctors in Manchester, it was vital there be a sign language interpreter available for the London appointment. I went to that appointment with my parents, it had to be difficult for them, but they were so supportive. I met several people there going through the same experience. and found it so interesting. I felt like part of a group. For the first time, I realised, I am not alone...

During my first appointment at GIC, Hammersmith, my name was called by the doctor. My parents prompted me, I stood up to go in, but there was no interpreter. I was disappointed and more than bit angry. It was clearly stated on the form that I needed a BSL interpreter. Instead of cancelling the appointment and since we travelled such a long distance, we went ahead with the appointment because I'd waited so long. My Dad supported me to facilitate communication.

This was not an easy thing for him to do. While he was the better signer between him and my mam. It was a mixture of embarrassment and anger that I had to impose upon him in this way to discuss such sensitive matters.

Forcing my dad to interpret made me so very angry! He was not keen on having to interpret but felt there was no choice. He already saw me suffer enough. I was angry because he should not have the extra responsibility. There was already enough on his plate without this added layer of complexity.

While many professionals ask family members to interpret, it is neither ethical nor acceptable. Interpreters are qualified communication professionals who have not only studied sign language, but also have extensive training in exactly how to interpret. Their most important qualification is impartiality. Their benefit is the fairness that comes from being unrelated to the deaf person other than through this professional relationship. There are clear professionally detached boundaries set in place.

Family members are supposed to be there for emotional support, not interpretation. So, I not only missed out having emotional support from my dad, this also put pressure on him to act as a professional interpreter. Instead of being a supportive father figure and digest the information from his own perspective, he had to concentrate on the doctor.

I remember one question from the doctor was, 'why have you decided you want to transition'? As any interpreter would do, he asked this question in the first person. For me, it was difficult to separate my dad from the doctor. It felt like my Dad was asking me all over again, like he had done long ago.

I could not separate him from the doctor and the question angered me. I vented my anger and frustration towards my dad, but it was through no fault of his own.

It was such a highly charged situation already, made even more traumatic through the lack of an interpreter.

To make it easy to understand, on a scale of 1 - 10, 1 - 5 would be a female range of hormones, and 6 - 10 would be the male range. I tested just below the male testosterone level, which means I was just barely in the female range. This meant I sort of had both sets of hormones. Because the doctor saw these results, he assumed I wanted to change from being female to male.

This was SO infuriating. Such a pivotal moment and the doctor could not even be bothered to read the case notes! It did not instil a great deal of faith or confidence in the hospital.

The doctor explained to my mam there was a possibility of me being intersex when she carried me. He said that could be the cause of my hormone levels being what were.

I had never heard that term before, so even I had to Google it myself! Intersex people are born with any of several variations in sexual characteristics including chromosomes, gonads, sex hormones or genitals. This helped put everything into perspective for my parents. To them there was a medical reason that suddenly made sense.

At the end of the consultation, I was so proud of my Dad for dealing with such a difficult and emotional situation. The doctor asked me if I wanted to change my identity and I responded, "yes, I did." He advised that I dress as the opposite sex for 2-3 years before he would allow me to start hormone replacement therapy.

I explained I had been wearing unisex clothes for a long time already. As a deaf person I can read faces and expressions very well and sense when someone is unsure.

I started to question myself. Something did not feel right. There was obviously some confusion, but he eventually realised I wanted to transition from boy to girl. The process though left me feeling furious with his confusion.

I felt the doctor was insulting me. But in hindsight, I now laugh about it. I had several clinic appointments in London over a long period of time, 3 to 4 years of travelling back and forth.

From this moment on I presented myself as a woman and was accepted at work in this way. They were so supportive, even allowing me to use the disabled toilet from the start. When I legally changed my name to Samantha, I was allowed to use the female toilets. I was advised by the GIC to change my name through the deeds poll for me to start hormones replacement therapy.

I asked mam and dad if they had had a baby girl, what name would they have chosen for her? Mam said, "Samantha Jayne." So, I took that name as a means to help me re-bond with my parents. I wanted the name to come from them just as if I had been born a girl. My name was legally changed by Deed Poll to Samantha Jayne Pearsall.

At work I used the female toilets. This solved another issue. Some of my male colleagues were not happy with me dressing as a female and using male toilets. The female staff had no problem with me using their toilet. It was not discrimination but more of a practical issue that needed resolving.

At the time I was working on the male unit of the hospital. I had a good rapport with these patients. They found it hard though to see me slowly transition to female. They did not really understand why. Some of them had complex mental health issues.

There was a forensic psychologist working on the ward who supported me and reinforced to patients that I was going through gender transition and reminded them to call me Samantha. This issue was also raised at the patients' monthly meeting. I felt a bit of tension in the air as they were finding it difficult to cope with the male me, they previously knew. Now they were trying to figure out why I was becoming a female. Some patients started to tease me. They thought it was funny. Luckily, I am quite thick skinned and kept reinforcing the boundaries they needed to adhere to. They accepted them quite well in the end.

I was also able to remove my personal feelings from situations, often with great difficulty! Luckily, I was able to understand how patients responded in the manner they did, and why. It stemmed back to their own childhood. I had to remember their reaction was not their fault. It was due to a lack of education.

So, I spent a lot of time teaching them empathy. We role played situations and I kept repeating the information in a way that was understandable for them. That perseverance paid off. We built good relationships in the end and they accepted me for who I was, Samantha.

The more I arrived at work as Samantha, the less they thought of me as Richard. They still recognised my sense of humour was the same, and my personality had not changed, just my appearance. I also know that at that time, I was not in a good mental state. Somehow working with them, I was able to suppress it, keep going and survive.

My friends reacted to my decision to transition with initial shock. They were quite upset and wondered if I was making the right decision. Quite naturally, they wanted to protect me.

I remember in the beginning my female friends would have hen parties or Ann Summers parties and I was not invited. That hurt. It took time for them to get used to me being a woman and realise I wanted to be involved in those events!

During the initial transition period, I was not accepted in either group. I also stopped being invited to gatherings of my male friends. So, I was caught in the middle of both groups and feeling left out.

Rusty was furious with how some of my friends treated me. I remember being so upset and crying to my mam I did not understand what I had done wrong and why I wasn't invited to belong to either group? Mam said, "no worries, these things take time."

This was partly why I escaped and moved to the Isle of Wight. It was easier not being around anyone. That way I did not have to feel rejection or the emotions I was already struggling with.

I remember when my mam introduced me to the extended family as Samantha for the first time. It felt awkward, partly because I was still battling with my own emotions. I was concerned about what they might think.

I don't have a cruel bone in my body. The last thing I ever want to do is upset anyone or damage relationships between my parents and our wider family. At first, I could feel the tension. And like with most new things, they just needed time to adjust to the new me. The more I saw of them, the more they forgot about Richard.

Overall, I felt so lucky they all responded with so much love and support. Sadly, some of my family members died before they got the chance to meet me as Samantha. However, I smile fondly when I think of them and I take great comfort in knowing they would be so proud. I strongly believe they are my guardian angels and no matter what happens?

They will always have my back.

11. GRIEVING RICHARD

*D*uring my transition, I met a man who was hearing. For confidentiality reasons, we'll call him Danny. We became partners and this added a whole new layer of confusion for my parents. They began questioning me. Was he gay or not?

This line of questioning greatly annoyed me. We ended up once in a big fight during which I confirmed he was straight and that we were happy together.

To explain further, as I changed my gender, I was now a woman. I identified with being a woman. I looked and dressed like a woman. And as a woman, I was attracted to straight males. Therefore, this was defined as a 'straight' relationship.

I am not attracted to gay men nor would they be attracted to me. I am a straight woman, so their type of relationship does not fit!

It's obvious if you think about it. The men I dated since transitioning have all... been... straight... They are attracted to women! I was naturally unsure about pursuing a relationship with bisexual men for one reason, I needed to feel confident they were not going to run off with another man! I experienced enough heartache. I could not cope with something like that happening!

I think my parents were still grieving over the loss of Richard as Samantha took over more control of my life. When mam and dad found out about me transitioning, they were devastated. They had lost their son. They mourned Richard and went through a long grieving process like someone had died. They knew they would never be able to see Richard as a man, ever again. And I could not really talk to them about it and advise them, because I had already been through enormous pain myself.

I struggled to understand their pain. Back then I thought they were just being difficult, deal with it! But I now understand. It was very emotionally draining for my parents and brothers. It was not the time to engage in a meaningful conversation about our emotions as there was just so much going on, there was no headspace for it.

A few months of me being with Danny, mam and dad met him for the first time. They were a bit uneasy about him. My mam tried to ask questions about Danny, but I got defensive thinking she was interfering. I would not answer. She found a way around it all, asking Rusty what he thought when I was out of the room. She knew by putting him on the spot he would give something away.

I kept my parents in the dark about Danny. I knew they wanted the best for me. They tried to be happy for me and did not let on their concerns about him. There was something about his timid behaviour around them, that caused their uncertainty. They were concerned he was gay or perhaps using me to satisfy some sort of fetish. They questioned if he was feeling genuine fondness for me.

They had seen me suffer so much throughout life the last thing they wanted was someone to hurt me. My dad would never want to give his daughter away to someone they did not feel was genuine. That's right, his daughter.

He now treated me like a daughter, totally different to how he treated Richard. Like the character Billy Bigelow in movie Carousel singing 'My Boy

Bill" and realising, "wait a minute, what if HE, is a girl?" And finishing the song talking about how important it is "to be a father to a girl…"

It was so nice for me to finally be comfortable in my own skin. When I first I became Samantha, my family treated me the way they treated Richard. Over time they gradually understood and treated me like a woman. This was new for everyone and it was all about taking time. While I struggled when they treated me like Richard, I spoke up. I became quite sassy, which is not in my nature. It all fuelled an anger deep within me. And it was not their fault.

One Christmas during my transition, my mam and dad bought me a David Beckham deodorant and aftershave set! I was so insulted. This was incredibly offensive. And it was not deliberate. They learned and would never make that mistake again! I gave the shaving set to Rusty!

That same Christmas, Rusty told his mam that I was now Samantha. She bought me a Charlie perfume set, which I thought was lovely. My dad never understood transgender until I went through the whole process, it really hit him as he learned more, and he now gets it.

He saw my pain and suffering. He felt strongly he wanted the right person for me, his daughter. Someone who is with me, for me. And not because of a fetish. My brother Matthew felt the same way. Matthew became super protective of me. I feel my dad was the role model there. He taught Matthew to be this way.

That still does not stop Matthew wanting to punch me sometimes! (I do like to wind him up because we are so close.) We have the same sense of humour, and we know what the other is thinking. And sometimes I can take things a step too far.

When I visited, the household became more argumentative. They were now trying to understand and really get their heads around what was happening and why I wanted to change my gender. I did not help the situation here. I was horrible and sassy. I did not really take on board how my parents were feeling.

They tried to explain how difficult it was for them. My hearing brother found it hard to accept. He mixed in a very "straight" circle of friends who had probably never encountered somebody like me before. My gay, deaf brother was fine, he already mixed with a diverse and multi-cultural group of people. Too, he had lived abroad in France and Corsica. My change of gender was never really a problem for him.

My parents had a dearth of support. This was not something that came up at the pub or in a church group. They had no signposts to check along the way for help. This all affected their relationship together as they constantly argued about me.

During this time, I dressed as a woman. My father found this increasingly difficult to cope with. He would often leave the house when I was there and visit a friend to avoid confrontation. The area I grew up in is economically deprived and insular. My mam grew concerned about how other extended family members would react to me.

The first time she dropped me off in the centre of Middlesbrough dressed as a woman to meet friends, she was terrified. The town centre was filled with typical north east "Yorkshire / Geordie" men. Richard could handle himself with this crowd, but could Samantha? I was annoyed with my Mam about this, felt she was overreacting and being too protective. In the end, I had a great night out and I came to no harm; Mam's fears were unfounded.

One funny moment when I stayed one weekend at my parent's home. I stupidly forgot to bring clean knickers with me. I told my Mam about it. She suggested I could borrow my Dad's boxer shorts. I thought she was joking, but she was not. I replied, "MAAAM, are you for real?!" I just could not get my head around what she was suggesting and wondered later if maybe she could not get her head around me asking to wear a pair of hers.

I texted Rusty, asked him to pop over to Morrison's and buy me some cheap knickers. He could not stop laughing when I told him what my Mam suggested. From time to time, he would make a joke about borrowing his boxer shorts if I did not bring any clean knickers with me.

My parents were still learning about the new me. Mam was really grieving. It felt like Richard had died. She would cry at work even though she had confidants that she could talk to. It affected her work as she could not concentrate.

Mam's boss noticed that all was not right, and she organised a meeting. Dad came to work that morning with Mam. They told her boss about my transition, which put everything into perspective. Mam's boss was incredibly supportive. She offered her counselling and even invited dad to take part in the counselling as well.

Things began to gradually improve for Mam and dad's relationship with each other and, indeed with me. Mam started calling me "Samantha" and I could see she was struggling. She wanted to see "Richard," but he was no longer there. So, the grieving was on-going.

Dad had problems saying "Samantha" as "Richard" still rolled naturally off his tongue. Dad had no one to talk with at work about my transition. He was now working in a very alpha male environment, on an oil rig in the North Sea.

My parent both learned coping strategies from the therapy around not being able to see their son anymore. Instead they now saw me as twins.

As my parents struggled to come to terms with all the new changes in my life, they were encouraged to think of Richard and Samantha as twins. This helped them let go of Richard and welcome me as Samantha.

They were sad to see Richard go, but so happy to see Samantha. It was a rebirth of their child too.

They brought Richard up and cared for him as a boy, bought him male clothes, deodorant, hair gel, razors, even colour schemes that were for a boy. They did all the things parents do with their sons. Suddenly, this person was gone and had been replaced. Their experience as parents shifted as I transitioned. This was something they had to adapt to as well.

My mam would now go out and buy me nail varnish, hair accessories, female deodorant, and items with girly colours like pink - something they had never experienced before. It was new for them to have a new daughter so much later in life.

My mam bought some hideous clothes for me and I had to say, "Mam that blouse is bloody awful!" She would get defensive and say, "well I'm trying Samantha, oh I can't do this!" And she would take it back to the shop.

I hugged her afterwards and apologised. Our tastes were just so different. She is more reserved whereas I am not afraid to wear something that is a little bit more revealing. But then we all are guilty of this transference. We buy things for others that we ourselves would like to wear. I felt though she was trying to dress me like Mrs. Doubtfire!

My entire life I could not show myself off. I was now proud of my achievement. My mam struggled to understand my choice in 'going out' clothes. She did not like low cut tops. And I am sure every mother has that battle with their daughters! When my mam would tell me to cover up, I would naturally do the opposite and pull my top further open to get a reaction. 'Stop it Samantha!' she would cry! While everything else about me had changed, my sense of humour did not.

My dad now changed into the protective father role. This was very new to him having raised three sons to fend for themselves. He was always affectionate however, became even more tender as time passed. Much more so than when I was Richard. I think partly it was due to me trying to be manly as Richard through football and sport. Now I was daddy's little girl, and maybe even more than a little spoiled!

Now I could live comfortably in my new identity.

12. HORMONES, TREATMENTS, AND THERAPIES GALORE!

*W*hilst I was still with Danny, I began my long-awaited hormone replacement therapy (HRT). This included large doses of the female hormone oestrogen. This is a medication I will need to take every day for the rest of my life.

Every four months for a year, I also had to receive injections to suppress the male hormones in my body. Too, there were laser treatment needed to remove my facial hair (which I had to self-finance because it was not funded by the NHS). I was also advised by my doctor to stop smoking because of the increased risk of heart attack linked to the HRT medication I was starting.

At the time I had a receding hair line which I naturally found difficult to cope with and could not yet afford a hair transplant. So, I used a lace wig which was glued onto my own hairline. This was so very painful a process to go through every three months. It made me cry because my hairdresser was rather rough plaiting my hair and did not realise how thin my hair was compared to other women who go through the same process. Danny used to say "don't be soft, be strong" which really annoyed me as I was the one going through the process, not him! I maintained this look for several years until I could afford a proper hair transplant.

While I appeared to be female, I was still a male. It felt wrong for me, but Danny liked it. It did not seem to present any problems as he liked trans females who had 'something extra'. It was like a fantasy for him.

I met him through an ordinary dating site, he was hearing but we were able to communicate. We took time to learn how to communicate with each other and over time, he developed signing skills naturally.

Danny left to work on an assignment in Shanghai for 6 months. This left me feeling bereft. I had been with him for about 3 years before the move. The job, he told me, was commission only and had to do with medical insurance. I continued to support him financially while he was there, paying for his accommodation and food. I needed to make sure he ate and had a roof over his head!

Living thousands of miles away, naturally I worried. He told me he was trying but did not manage to earn much of anything. I really felt badly for him. He was trying very hard to achieve something. I really wanted that for him. While he was there though, I felt out of control.

I could not look after him on the other side of the world, so I did the best I could. We chatted every other day, but the time difference made it difficult. Shanghai is 7 or 8 hours ahead of UK time and does not observe Summertime, so their clocks never moved, but ours did. When I spoke to him in the morning here, it was teatime there, 4:00-5:00 pm.

I always put others first. That means I often forget myself. I did not want to prevent him from achieving his dreams. I also felt the adage, 'absence makes the heart grow fonder' would work in our case and our love would grow stronger. And it did work at the time. We stayed together but it was difficult for me, not having the direct emotional support and connection.

Danny returned home from Shanghai after 8-months. I did not have the money to pay for his flight home, so my parents again stepped in and bought his ticket. Things just did not work out well for him over there. By now he also knew I was moving to the Isle of Wight and he decided that he wanted to be with me.

While he was away, the only way I could make time pass quickly was to throw myself into my work. So, I worked a lot of overtime hours to pass the time. I was also experiencing a high level of stress. There were changes at work, within my own body, my partner was away, and I had to both self-finance the flat as well as try to fund cosmetic changes by and for myself.

I decided to relinquish my permanent post at the hospital and become bank staff. I could choose the hours I wanted to work, as the constant hospital shifts were too much for me to cope with. I needed to be careful and look after myself. Yet I felt weak, had a loss of concentration, and depression returned, due to my loss of energy.

Giving up my flat meant I moved around a couple of times and lived with friends. This meant paying less rent. It all gave me time to reflect and decide what I wanted to do with my life.

13. EVERY SUMMER WE CAN RENT A COTTAGE ON THE ISLE OF WIGHT

F eeling I needed something closer to my healthcare and deaf roots, I applied for a new job and moved to the Isle of Wight. There I became the Deputy Manager of a care home for elderly deaf residents. I thought a new life, new partner, new workplace would mean a completely fresh start.

The night before I was due to move south, I felt sick. Was I making the right decision to move? The thoughts of leaving my family and friends behind, hiring a van full of our belonging (including fluff the cat), driving through the night to catch the last ferry from Southampton to Cowes. Moving into an apartment above Gibbs & Gurnells on Union Street opposite a Wetherspoons, terrified me.

I needed to put myself first. I needed a period of self-reflection. I saw an advert for a Deputy Manager of a Deaf care home. Even though I had a job with a steady income, I thought I would grab this opportunity. I ran away from home, family, and friends and completely revamped my life.

I needed time to process everything that happened and... I needed to heal. I studied and achieved a higher education management NVQ diploma while on the island. There was so much I wanted to achieve in life but had to be patient and do it one step at a time. I wanted to change things for the better. I lived on the island for three years and realised it was one of the best decisions I ever made. I would not be in the position I am today without those life experiences.

Island life was quiet and relaxing. A perfect place to sit and reflect. I lived in a 'penthouse' and daily watched the sea. Every other Saturday I would see Cunard's RMS Queen Mary II set sail for New York. I would also watch catamarans and the hovercraft head off to Portsmouth. I was in a prime location, opposite the Ryde pier. The island was too small for normal trains, so they used old London Tube carriages instead. They travelled from the end of the pier to Ryde station, a mere 745 yards!

I did not feel trans when I was there, I felt like a woman. I loved that feeling. No one was there to remind me of my previous gender. I did not socialise much. My time out of work was spent with Danny, exploring island life. It was great for a short period, but I could not stay there. I am a city girl at heart, and I need to be kept busy.

I felt a lot better and things were going well for the first time in my life.

I continued to travel to London for clinic appointments in preparation for my surgery. I repeatedly had to reinforce my need for an interpreter, the added frustration being whether that interpreter would show up.

In my new workplace many of the residents and staff were unaware of my new gender. This made me feel more normal as nobody knew. The Isle of Wight was not as 'with it' as London.

I felt I could get on with my life in a normal way, experience, and enjoy island life. It gave me time to reflect. Although I still felt exhausted, a little unwell at times, was still becoming thinner and did not know why... I thought it was just the stress I was going through.

Working in a care home, I was deeply passionate about supporting Deaf elderlies.' Nobody knew I was trans on the island until the last few months before I relocated back to Manchester. I worked the hours God sent me, ate well, slept, and studied every day. It felt like 'Groundhog Day' days.

When I received the news about my sister-in-law being pregnant and my brother expecting his first child, I was over the moon and so happy for them! At the same time, I was also emotional. I wanted a baby of my own, and I knew I would never be able to have my own biological child.

I remember working the night shift when the news came that my first nephew was born in September. It was 2014 and I was absolutely delighted to be an auntie. My mam facetimed me to share the news! While I was full of joy for my brother and sister-in-law, I also felt hurt and heartbroken. Mam could sense the pain and saw it in my eyes. I could not hide it. It was such a mixture of emotions and the reality was I felt so far removed from that.

Too, my relationship with Danny was on the verge of breakdown. We were not happy together, although that is all I really wanted as well. I was so far away. Because I could not be there physically, I was also terribly upset.

I think now it was a good thing to be away. It gave me time to absorb the situation and confront the feelings it stirred up and try to make sense of them. I had to nurture my mind and wellbeing.

I was still smoking heavily even though I was taking the HRT. Danny continually tried to reinforce that this was a dangerous thing to do. The doctor at the hospital told me if I did not give up smoking, the surgery would need to be cancelled. This was said in a kind way, but unfortunately to no effect.

I asked them to give me a definitive date for the surgery, which would have encouraged me to give up smoking. They could not give me any idea of dates. So, I rebelliously thought, what was the point of giving up something I enjoyed and was a release for me both physically and emotionally?

Part Three

BECOMING SAMANTHA

Oh yes, I am wise
But its wisdom born of pain
Yes, I've paid the price
But look how much I gained
If I have to, I can do anything
I am strong
I am invincible
I am woman

I AM WOMAN

HELEN REDDY, 1971

14. 'THE' DAY ARRIVES

I could never go alone to my hospital appointments in London because I could not depend on there being an interpreter available. So, I had to rely on Danny coming with me. For at least 50% of my appointments, there was no interpreter present. Several there were unqualified or did not have relevant experience. I kept stressing the importance of continuity, having the same interpreter whenever possible, because they would be more aware of my medical history.

During this time period, I was also supporting a deaf friend of mine who was going through the same gender reassignment surgery at the same hospital. My friend had similar interpreter issues but no family support. They were all deaf and therefore could not assist with communication. This made me realise how important it would be for me to have an interpreter the day of my operation.   My friend went home after successful surgery. I continued to support her, and we have become exceptionally good friends. She, became my 'sister from another mister.'

Finally, in August of 2013, I received a letter from the hospital. My surgery was set for the 12th of December. I remember that day so clearly. I had finished work. It was a lovely day and I was walking down the High Street towards the beach. I saw Danny coming towards me, letter in hand. I read it, incredulously.

This was the best news of my life and I immediately threw away the cigarette I had in my hand. It was the last one I would ever have!

On my days off, I explored the island. I visited many different places and discovered from my parents that my Mam's relatives who used to live in Kent had moved onto the island. It was something I did not know and least expected. It was so nice to have that connection again, bringing back all the memories I had with them.

I also concentrated on learning to drive. I needed to pass my driving test before the surgery. (I passed.)

For my first 18-months on the Isle, nobody knew I was transgender. It felt so wonderful and lovely that I was just Samantha. I loved the anonymity and needed this time to really heal.

But I also noticed Danny started to drink more, shortly after moving onto the island. Once the surgery was booked and looming, he drank even more frequently. Danny was financially dependent on me. He was technically self-employed but did not bring in any money. I remember saying to him, even if he brought home a few pounds a week, it would help.

He felt he was too overqualified to do just any job like a taxi driver or working at McDonald's. He eventually got a job as a taxi driver, but after a few weeks quit because he did not like it. He also did not claim any benefits because he relied on me. I really wanted some financial help but did not get any. He helped sometimes, but for most of the relationship he did not work. It was both unequal and exhausting.

He often went to the pub across the road where he would sit alone and drink, reading a newspaper. I was responsible for paying all the bills. I worked around the clock to support us financially and studied. It was not reciprocated.

I remember I wanted to get my nails done, but Danny said no, we could not afford it. Plus, he hated acrylic nails and, to be fair, the Isle of

Wight was not that type of place. Danny said this even though he spent my money going to the pub!

It disappointed me. I wished he would try harder. He would buy branded clothing such as adidas but told me to buy second-hand clothes from the charity shop.

One time when we were in London, he mentioned, in front of mam, I should go to Kensington charity shops. It was an affluent area so there would be designer clothes in the shops there. My mam and dad did not say anything at the time as they did not want to interfere in our relationship, but they were furious. They thought I deserved better for all the hard work I did.

They said to me "you spend hours working so hard to make ends meet no wonder you are mentally and physically burnt out." I am such a positive person, but I think I am too optimistic sometimes. I would always tell myself; it'll be better next year.

The first Christmas Danny and I were together, he bought me an iPhone. The following 5 Christmases we spent together. He did not get me anything. He once bought me a pair of earrings, but that was with my own money!

Rusty worked out that I spent an obscene amount of money supporting Danny. It was nearly £45,000, which I was embarrassed to admit. I felt, no, I feel so foolish looking back that I did not realise it at the time. I guess love is blind. And in the process, I learned "money can't buy me love."

I never once asked for a penny back because I felt he went through enough trouble himself. Maybe I am too kind. I wanted to leave things as they were without creating a stir.

When I moved back to Manchester and started working for a charity for people with complex needs, I underwent domestic abuse training. It opened my eyes and woke me up. While I do not think it was Danny's intention, I realised what was being described in the course, was the situation I lived in. I realised then and there, I had to walk away.

Relationships always were a steep learning curve for me. I learned I will not put up with it again or give things away too easily. It is a hard lesson to learn when you're in love.

The night before my surgery we went to London. My dad was working in Aberdeen and could not get the time off. My Mam though booked a week off work, as did Danny. They stayed together in an apartment in Hammersmith and the three of us went for a meal together.

I remember packing my bag for the hospital. I do not know why, but on the way to the hospital I asked Danny how he felt about my imminent surgery. He was flabbergasted I asked him how he felt, mostly because I had never asked him that question during all the time, were together.

He said, he did not really want me to have the operation and reminded me the psychiatrist said it could affect our relationship...but I trivialised it and took no notice of what he said. I also realised I should have asked him ages ago. Even if I did, and he gave me that same response I would still have gone ahead with the surgery anyways. While some may see that as selfish, it was way beyond time for me to take care of myself...

When I arrived at hospital, I was taken to the Marjory Warren ward. They admitted me. There were about six of us going through the same operation the next day. I remembered wanting a pizza the night before, but Danny said, "you are not allowed to eat before the surgery." The nurse was quite insistent that I could not leave the hospital. She finally relented when I became adamant and I was allowed to go across the road to the Pizza Express.

My mam and Danny went back to the flat. I stayed overnight in the hospital preparing for the surgery. That is when the enormity of it all hit me. The thought of Danny's remark was running through my head. I could not talk to anyone on the ward because of my deafness. So, I lay there looking at the clock. I just wanted the surgery to be over with so I can live my life again.

The nurse told Mam that I would be first on the list because of the interpreter provision. I woke up in the morning feeling nervous; they prepared me for surgery, with the usual gown and stockings. That was when it hit me. My mam was not there. Danny had not yet arrived. I asked the nurse if we could wait for them, but she said theatre was waiting for me. I texted them both to tell them I was going down to theatre., I tried a number of delaying tactics, washed my face, went to the toilet... and the nurse was becoming more and more frustrated with me. There was a schedule to stick to. Danny arrived, I gave him a kiss and cuddle. He said Mam was on her way but was struggling on her dodgy knee. He was not allowed to come into theatre, only my interpreter was allowed.

I remember walking out of the ward and just as I was about to go down the stairs, to my right. I saw my mam in the distance and quickly ran to and kissed her. Mam asked me the final question if I was sure I wanted to go ahead. I angrily replied, "of course, I'm not going to change my mind."

15. SWEET RELIEF, ELATION & HOME

W hen I woke up after the operation, I looked at the clock. It was 11.15. I remember seeing the interpreter who told me I was in the recovery room. It felt like I had only been asleep for 15-minutes or so when in fact, the operation took two hours and was a complete success.

As I was taken back to the ward, I felt simultaneously elated and angry. I questioned why I had not done this years ago. When the doors opened, I saw Mam and Danny standing in the distance waiting. Mam burst into tears. I said, "don't be stupid I'm fine." That, unfortunately, is my way of blocking my own emotion by saying "I'm fine" when in fact I could cry... but not in front of Mam.

As soon I got out of the theatre, I appeared a little drowsy. I could not feel my legs and mam started to panic. She thought something had gone wrong (she tends to overreact). The nurse told me I had a spinal epidural which was why I could not feel my legs. I would have to wait for the anaesthetic to ease off.

I stayed in the hospital for a week. I had the same interpreter come in every day. This is because the interpreter was now an issue I was forced to escalate to a formal complaint to PALS (the NHS Patient Advice and

Liaison Service). This was when they realised how importance is it for me to have same interpreter throughout all my appointments.

I was bored laying in hospital for that week. Being deaf, I had no one to talk to. My dad flew down from Aberdeen to London to visit me. He was very emotional, and I think a bit surprised I had actually gone ahead with the surgery. (There was no going back now.)

Dad said I needed to get out of bed and go for walks... so we went to the Costa Coffee shop based in the hospital. The walk took forever, and I was terribly slow. I must have looked like John Wayne when he climbs down off his horse!

After I woke from the surgery, I was being wheeled on my bed to the ward for recovery. I saw my mam gasp. She covered her mouth with her hands and burst into tears.

She said that was the hardest day for her. She knew there was no going back, and Richard was definitely gone now. She felt joy and pain simultaneously. Danny was standing next to my mam. I sensed he was putting on a brave face, He did not say much, however, he told me he was off to get some food from McDonald's which was about a 15-minute walk from the hospital.

When he said that, even through the drowsiness and anaesthetic, I sensed something was not right. He did not embrace me, kiss me, hug me, or look happy to see me.

The medications blocked any feelings about Danny's reaction, it took me 24 years of struggle and battle to get to this point. I deserved happiness. I have never experienced such elation or feeling of freedom. When I woke up, it felt I had a new lease on life. I was born again as a new person and every stress completely disappeared. The slate was totally wiped clean and there was nothing that could stop me. I felt invincible. It was like a boost of adrenaline. I was floating so light and free, without a care in the world. It was the best feeling I ever had.

I would love to go back and do it all again. Even with the Physical pain, I would do it again without a shadow of a doubt. I was in heaven. It was wonderful. I struggle to put it back then into words. Imagine if, as a heavy smoker you did not have a cigarette for a week. Then that first puff and with that long drag instantly all the stress just melted away.

Now multiply that length of time by 24 years, and you might begin to understand how I felt. I knew my relationship with Danny would go downhill. The surgery reaction showed there was nothing that would keep him happy. And if my main focus was to make him happy, then I would be unhappy... but all for his gain not my own.

I was so dosed up on morphine, it made me feel nauseous. I had never been on drugs in my life and it was not agreeing with me! It was so bad, I persuaded the nurse to take me off it saying, "if she didn't, I would the drip line out!"

My transgender friend I previously supported came to visit me with her deaf family which was lovely! We all had a nice chat in the visitor room. Visiting hours were normally strictly between the hours of 6 and 8pm but I knew how to play the 'deaf' card, explaining I was isolated and needed the extra visiting time to enable people to come and see me. Too, I have always thought 'if you don't ask, you don't get'.

It was nearing Christmas, so we watch the 'X Factor' in the visitor room. This was the year Sam Bailey won. The ward was all decorated. It had a 'Christmassy' feel. I felt it was already Christmas. I had been given the best present ever! I signed to Mam to tell that to the surgeon, he laughed joyously!

I went through several clinical procedures for a full week to clean the wound. After this I thought I was discharged. So, I texted my dad to come and pick me up. I said my goodbyes to the other patients, left a thank you card and chocolates for the nurses, and left with my Mam, Dad and Danny.

Later that afternoon Mam received a phone call while we were in the car. 'Where's Samantha,' they asked. Mam said, 'she's here with me'. The nurse said that I was not supposed to have left. I had discharged myself earlier than I should have. I should have waited for medication and discharge information.

The nurses agreed to post everything to me at my parent's house where I was staying for my recuperation. We all had a laugh in the car.

Following instructions, a consistent problem for Richard, now afflicted Samantha!

16. CHRISTMAS, DEJA VU ALL OVER AGAIN

I remember arriving home, seeing the Christmas tree, and feeling incredibly happy. For the next two weeks I felt like the Queen. I was waited on hand and foot, never having to lift a finger for myself.

After recovering in hospital for a week, it was time to recuperate at home. I was advised to take 6 months off of work. I knew I would recover better at home than on the Isle. When you are ill you just want that soothing comfort of your parents' love and attention. I knew my parents would care for me and nurture me. That's all I wanted. It was Christmas time. So, I enjoyed being with family.

I remember mam and dad hiring a car to get us back to the North East since dad had flown down from Aberdeen and mam took the train. The car journey from London to Middlesbrough took about 5 or 6 hours with a break to allow for movement and circulation. I sat on a foam ring which protected my new vagina from touching the seat as it was all quite sore, sensitive, and needed time to heal.

Fresh out of hospital, I was cuddled up with Danny in the back for comfort. My dad drove and my mam sat in the front. He was the designated driver since he could cope with busy London traffic. My mam could not!

As soon as we arrived home, Danny created distance between us. It was like he was handing responsibility back to my parents. He seemed to be 'tolerating' the situation. It was obvious this was not where he wanted to be. He did not say much at all and spent most of his time isolated in the bedroom where he loved to drink.

I don't want to paint him in a bad light, but I do have a memory on New Year's Eve, I was all dressed and dolled up, excited to ring in the New Year ahead and celebrate the new me with him. The reality was vastly different. He got so drunk he did not make it to 12. He was fast asleep in bed, so I celebrated alone while my family was over in the pub.

I could not yet leave the house. I was still in so much pain from the surgery. I watched the tv and the famous London fireworks on my own and headed off to bed shortly thereafter.

The following morning, I gave him a piece of my mind. It did not go down well! I told him his behaviour was very selfish. He disagreed. I did not have to say anything to my mam and dad, they knew. They always read me so well. Their long-held reservations about him were now on full display for the entire family to see.

For most of the 6 months convalescence, I was downstairs chatting away with my beloved family and watching shows like the Real Housewives of Orange County (which my dad hated). He kept asking why I was watching this 'scripted shite?' The programme was so corny and cheesy. But I loved it.

I watched the full series while my parents were at work. It was so comfortable and lovely to be able to stay with them. It felt like home. Danny often walked to the local shop alone, and visited the local pub for a pint and a newspaper while I stayed home. This was Danny's daily routine.

My parents, and Danny would run a bath for me every single night, filling it with salt and warm water to heal my wounds. I felt so sad Danny could not share in the excitement with me. This was devastating and heart-breaking. I tended to tear up in the bath thinking about this.

The first time I got in the bath with my open wound, I looked down in anticipation and gasped, but it was a lovely gasp. It was a beautiful feeling to no longer have something horrible dangling between my legs. I thought this is what I should have been born with and not had to suffer for 24 years! There was a real burning sensation and I was quite sore! But at the same time, it was worth it. The feeling was surreal and put my mind at ease.

Going to the toilet was a new experience. I had to relearn how to pee. Men stand and ladies sit, so sitting was new to me. I remember crouching over the toilet in the most awkward position, to marvel at this new way of passing water. It took practice and some getting used to as I was fascinated.

I also had to stay in my room 2-3 times per day for an hour to dilate my vagina using a Vaginal Dilator. This stretched the vaginal hole. If this was not done, it would close up and cause many other problems. This regimen continued for 6 months, slowly reducing over time.

Some of my local friends came to visit me at my parents' home. It was so nice to see them and be able to talk about the surgery I'd been through. They were so happy and thrilled it all went so well.

Later that day, Rusty came to visit me and we had loads to talk about with things that happened in London and my surgery. I was in the kitchen brewing tea. My mam came in and told me to not show off my designer vagina because it would not be a very ladylike thing for me to do. I started laughing and said, "Mam! the more you tell me what to do, I will naturally do the opposite," whilst smirking.

My Mam was trying to coach me how to "walk and to talk and to act like a lady" to Quote My Fair Lady. In my head, I was already a lady, but her perspective was quite different. Therefore, it bugged me sometimes.

When I was being 'challenging,' my mam would respond, "Oh Samantha!" and storm off into the living room.

Rusty came into the kitchen, we got talking briefly about my surgery and how it went. He was checking his phone while I was making our tea. I could not resist it as I want to show him my new lady garden, because I was so over the moon with it. I was smiling like the Cheshire Cat. As always, I took no notice of what my Mam was saying.

As soon as Rusty turned to face me, I showed him my brand-new vagina. He looked gobsmacked and bewildered. I was not sure of his reaction. Nevertheless, he then said, "Oh that looks rather swollen, but splendid and... it's not my cup of tea darling," he then cackled.

I had no intention of being rude and it wasn't about flaunting it. I was bursting with pride. Something I had to fight so hard to get, I wanted to show off for a change. That lasted only for a short period. I can assure you, dear reader, that I do not go around doing that now! I admit that would not be a very ladylike thing to do!

Because Danny and I had a non-existent sex life, the motivation for me to dilate started to wear thin. I neglected to do it as often as I should have. Today, I am in a position where it has closed slightly, and I am near to the point where I might need surgery again. I just cannot be bothered with it now. I could try and dilate again, but I may have left it a little too late.

There have been several traumatic events in my life. Christmas seems to always be a really upsetting time for me. Three Christmases ago, I remember the family was gathered at my parents' house. Mam and dad exchanged gifts, as did Phillip and his husband Celso, as did Matthew and his wife Katie. I looked around and there was no one for me to exchange gifts with and I felt heartbroken. I felt left out. I wanted to experience what they all had.

It might have come across as me being spoiled but it is not about the presents. It is much deeper than that. It cut me to the core and was painful. Watching the John Lewis adverts on tv, you always see the 'perfect' couple. They romanticise what Christmas should look like and be. You never see adverts with young singles at Christmas!

Every Christmas morning, my mam asks me if I'm ok. It triggers me immediately and I cannot help but cry. Then I feel as if I am ruining Christmas! I know it is all part of the healing process, I'll get there eventually, and I have always tried to be positive about everything. But sometimes emotions get in the way.

I want to love someone and be loved. I am a very loving person and I have so much love to give. Looking around at my family was triggering to me. I thought, what have I done to deserve this? I have grown up seeing couples, regardless of gender, who appear to be in happy relationships and marriages. It has always been what I imagined my future would hold and is what I want.

I think my family only just realised how much it affected me last year. I was tired and my emotions got the better of me. My parents realised at that point that things needed to change. They fully empathised. Last Christmas things really improved, my mam filled bags full of bits and bobs of gifts for me, which seemed to fill that void.

Yet again I was a little spoiled. I have been on this emotional roller-coaster my whole life. Why am I so different from my family? Everyone says, one day you will meet Mr Right when the time is right. And my unspoken response is... I do not want to wait until I'm 60!

I want to meet someone now while I'm young and enjoy our lives and grow old together. I see young women in the street with their boyfriends and I long for that. I do not feel that level of equality yet. I feel being trans is an additional barrier and will make it more difficult to find someone who will accept me for who I am.

17. BACK TO MANCHESTER

After about a year of working in the care home on the Isle of Wight, I was chatting to my colleagues about where Danny and I were from. It turned out one of the staff had grown up in the same village as Danny. Now there's a coincidence, I thought.

As we discussed further, this person grew up with Danny! I couldn't believe it. I was shocked! I wanted to get away with not knowing anyone here, but it certainly did not work out that way.

What a small world. I told Danny when I got home from work. He could not believe it either! They met and had a catch up. Danny and I socialised with work colleagues once in a blue moon. But I think because of my position as a Deputy Manager, I was also wary about Danny having one too many drinks.

I faced a real dilemma of whether I should tell everyone about my past. I decided to open about who I was. With the connection of Danny's friend from Manchester, I did not want them to find out from someone else. There is no point in hiding, people always find out in the end.

My cousin from Kent also lived on the island. She found out and offered to support me with any help if needed. She looked after my cat while I was away recuperating.

Work colleagues were also very understanding once I came out. When I had the surgery, they gave me 6 months off with full pay! I was in a much stronger position than I had been when I arrived.

I was mentally well, made the decision to move back to Manchester, and I knew that it was the right time. I wanted to move back to the place where I first came out. I was back to my old self and I was going to return with confidence and strength.

Manchester was bustling with opportunity. It was my home. It felt like a safety net. I planned the return and knew we would eventually split up. We ended things and I moved in with Rusty. We lived together before I moved to the Isle of Wight. And he had moved back to his mam's in Middlesbrough. When I asked him if he would like to move back in together, he leaped at the chance.

He knew the opportunities were so much better in Manchester. The quality of life there is amazing. It holds a special place in our heart as it was where we first moved in together in 2008. Our lives began together here.

Part Four

WISDOM
BORN OF PAIN

You can bend but never break me
'Cause it only serves to make me
More determined to achieve my final goal
And I come back even stronger
Not a novice any longer
'Cause you've deepened the conviction in my soul
I am woman watch me grow
See me standing toe to toe
As I spread my lovin' arms across the land
But I'm still an embryo
With a long, long way to go
Until I make my brother understand

I AM WOMAN

HELEN REDDY, 1971

18. ZERO BUYER'S REMORSE

I hoped the surgery would make me happier living in my own skin. It did. I felt at peace in my new body.

It was an exceptionally long recovery. I stayed at my parents for about six months. It was a struggle at times, as the post-operative care was often painful and drawn out. It was exhausting for me.

Eventually, I was discharged from all hospital care and carried on with my normal working life.

I went through another bout with depression as it became clear I would soon need to end things with Danny. We fought often and were too often at loggerheads regarding further cosmetic procedures I wanted, especially a hair transplant, which was VERY expensive. As usual, in the end I won the argument! I am not the type of person who gives up easily.

I had a consultation with Farjo, a hair transplant centre in Manchester. They explained I could have a Follicular Unit Transplantation or FUT procedure. This was where they took hair from the back of my head and transplanted it to the front. This required 12-hours of surgery, all in one day and under light sedation. Thankfully, I could not feel a thing and it was not uncomfortable at all. Post-operatively I required continuous hair care. Thankfully, the transplant was remarkably successful, and hair started to grow within six months. This boosted my confidence as I no longer needed hair extensions or to cover a receding hairline. I felt much happier.

Because of the move back to Manchester, I was becoming my own person. But, typically, I can never have enough surgery and I investigated getting a breast augmentation. I booked a consultation and went ahead with that expensive surgery.

Since the breast augmentation, I was now more confident. I felt 100% like a woman now. Too, I now had nights out numerous times with my friends, something I did not have for a few years before my breast augmentation surgery.

I went to a beauty parlour in Prestwich and had my make-up done. I was not an expert at doing make-up by myself. The more times I went there, my make-up skills vastly improved. I watched and learned from the staff how to apply it and which products to use. This included advice and tips by Paige Louise who I initially told I was a transgender and struggling with how to do my make-up. She reassured me she would do everything she could to help me gain confidence. Paige who is now a well-known make-up artist, went into collaboration with other famous artists. She always put me at ease and showed me how to do make-up skilfully.

I contacted the Cirumed Clinic in Marbella to see if I could have a Brazilian Butt Lift. That procedure involved transferring fat from my stomach into the back of my buttocks to enhance the curve. I flew down to the clinic for the surgery. It went very well.

I also eventually had a second procedure which made my curve more feminine. I couldn't thank enough the work Dr Aslani did for me. I would go back in the future to have procedures done. The Cirumed Clinic is amazing, very professional and, most importantly, the staff are so very welcoming, and the clinic is spotlessly clean.

Later that year, I flew to Antalya, Turkey to have my teeth crowns done at Turkey Dental Excellence. I had 28 crowns implanted which was another great decision. It boosted my confidence and was my final cosmetic procedure. My transition was now complete.

Where previously I focused on myself and where 'I' needed to be personally, I began to see more of my friends and family. For the first time in my life, I was fully content. Home was where I could be my true self.

I did not mourn the loss of Richard in that moment. I never even considered him, to be honest. It is only now when I look back at photos, that I see Richard. I love looking at those old childhood photos and reminisce. I was such a cute little boy.

Looking at photos from my teenage years really hurts. I see a grown Richard in so much emotional pain and feel so sorry for him. I know what he went through and I would not wish that pain and uncertainty on anyone. While I feel somewhat detached when I look, I remind myself that that is me. I could never go back and live the life Richard lived again. While I suffer pain as Samantha, and went through many traumas, nothing compares to what Richard went through. I look back at myself as that little boy and feel proud of how far I have come.

My parents still have photos on their wall of me as a boy. I would never ask them to take them down or deny them that pleasure. My childhood was amazing and is full of fond memories of our global family holidays to Canada to visit extended family and Orlando.

There is one picture on the wall I am not too keen about. It was me as a teenager. Although I can tolerate it because it lives in an area of the house that is not used very much, the top corner of the stairs, I do not like that constant reminder of where I was during that time. It is hard to look back on being a teenager because of the struggles I battled through. Sometimes though, I take a quick peek. It also reminds me of how far I have come.

Thanks to my newfound confidence and complete healing, I decided it was time to move away from the Isle of Wight. I applied for a job in

Manchester. I wanted to be closer to my family and I was about to become an auntie. My nephew was about to be born.

I packed everything up and got on the car ferry back to the mainland (we Islanders called the main British Island, the Mainland). After a few hours of driving north, I was able to reflect on what I went through over the last three years. Living on the island helped me accurately think about all the time spent away from friends and family. It did though help me build up my health and strength. I was ready to face the reality of this new chapter of my life in Manchester.

19. BREAKING UP

From day one, I met Danny as Samantha. It was clear on my dating profile that I was trans so there were no surprises for anyone. His dating profile stated that he was straight.

I fancied him straightaway. I was really attracted to him. He had a skinhead and I do not know why. I don't have a specific type, but I do have a thing for men who look rough and ready. I don't mind a couple of scars either or a wonky nose.

He was a little taller than me. I do like tall men. I think it is because someone who appears that way makes me feel safe. They can protect me. In truth, I know that is not the case, but it is what I imagine when I see people who fit that description. I like a man who's strong, confident, and dominant, someone who can handle me.

As soon as we met, I made it clear that I was not happy with this foreign object that was attached to my body and it was my intention to get rid of it. I do not think he realised how determined I was and how stubborn I could be. When I told him, I wanted to get rid of it, he did not react much. I felt safe in the comfort it did not bother him.

Looking back, maybe deep down he thought I would never go through with it. When I asked him how he felt about my upcoming surgery, he momentarily paused and did not say a word, his face appeared to be frozen. I got the impression that he was less than elated with this surgery, but he decided to support me. He said, the night before surgery, he would prefer me to keep the genitals that I was born with. A little too late there Danny boy.

It seemed clear that he wanted me to keep it for his own benefit in the bedroom. He wanted his cake and eat too. He never considered what I needed or wanted when it came to my transition or what was good for my mental wellbeing. Throughout the entire surgery process, I barely had a word of reassurance, support, or comfort from Danny.

My relationship with Danny was now on the verge of collapse. It had been declining since immediately after my surgery. Our sex life disappeared as soon as I got rid of my manhood. Danny became more of a carer for me post-surgery at my parents' house. When we returned to the Isle of Wight, this carer vs. lover status continued.

He picked up my medication, cooked my tea for when I got home from work, washed my clothes, sorted out the post and was a good house husband. While I must admit he did a lot for me around the house, we were more friends than lovers. I felt my lover had left and there was a distance between us. I still wanted intimacy but for Danny, things had changed. That really hurt. But I could not change what he thought.

Danny and I moved back to Manchester. I had a plan worked out, but honestly knew a couple of months post-surgery, it was not going to work out.

I fought to keep the relationship alive and make it work but admitted defeat in the end. It was 3 years before we completely ended it. I knew separating from Danny in the Isle of Wight would be too risky. I had no support network, nothing, or anyone to fall back on.

Post-surgery, I started to question Danny's sexuality. He was not attracted to my genitals anymore, so I wondered if he might be gay? I had my doubts and did not want that uncertainty. I broached the subject about going our separate ways in Danny's house. He rented it while we were in the Isle of Wight and it is where we first went when we returned to Manchester.

I had been covering the mortgage payments as well as our rent. I said that it was not going to work, and he agreed. He did not fight for me; I think in some ways I did him a favour because he did not have to do it for himself.

I wanted different things from life. We had been together for six years and had been through quite a lot. I just wanted to get on with my new life and so Danny and I agreed to just be friends. In the end, we both wanted different things.

The biggest issue the whole time I was with Danny was I went through a lot of changes and had never experienced what it was like to be a fully independent woman. I wanted to explore that, and he agreed.

In hindsight, I remembered the psychologist said (and was reminded by Danny the night before my surgery) our relationship would likely not last because of the surgery. I had not really taken that on board at the time. Now though, it was true. He was right.

We felt out of place in Middlesbrough. I loved Danny so very much, but I knew that this could not continue and that I needed to let him go. I still love Danny, every time his name is mentioned, I well up. Still now. It is heart wrenching.

Love is the most powerful thing in the world. I had to cut ties with him completely after separating because it pulled on my heart strings and messed with my head every time we were in touch.

After we split up, we kept in touch for another 3 years. I stopped the financial support and he did not ask for any either. For the first time in my life I felt rich. I had money to go on holidays. I travelled around the world, went clubbing, got my hair and nails done, went out for meals, and treated myself to a brand-new Mercedes GLA Premium 4-wheel drive in black.

It was a stupid impulse purchase. Rusty advised me not to buy a car without him there. He knows cars very well. He was right, I bought it and its guzzled petrol like there was no tomorrow! I eventually got rid of it and bought my Fiat 500 which I loved. It is so nippy and great for driving around the city. I much preferred it to the Mercedes, and it felt so good to have financial freedom,

I felt like I got my life back. Keeping in touch with Danny was the most difficult thing we could have done. It would have kept things alive between us. We could not move on; we could not get closure.

He would check in to see how I was doing; I would do the same. Every few months we would see each other and spend some time together. It was all purely platonic. There was no physical contact between us at all. We loved each other, that did not change. That was the hardest thing to come to terms with.

It was a constant battle between my mind and emotions. Enough was enough, and after 2 and a half years of turmoil just maintaining a friendship, I put an end to it all for my own sanity.

Rusty saw how much seeing Danny affected me. He hated seeing it. He saw it from a different perspective. He felt Danny treated me a bit like a puppet and that he was manipulating me, saying things that pulled me down. He would come round to drop off letters and Rusty knew how I would feel after he left.

He felt Danny blamed me for leaving him. He told those close to us both that when I had my breast implants, I ended things. He took no responsibility at all for the breakdown of the relationship and this frustrated Rusty. He resented the fact that I was financially supporting Danny. He did not say anything to begin with, because it was nothing to do with him. And as time went on, he told me what he thought, as my best friend who wanted to protect me.

I made the decision to cut all ties once and for all. A new home, a blank page, a fresh start. I am still very fond of him and I wish we could be friends. And I can see we could, but it is too heart-breaking, and I could not handle it.

Even though I may disagree with the things he did, love is love. I know I cannot get back with him because I changed my genitalia. The sexual attraction was no longer there for him, even though I still felt the same as I always did for him.

We ended it because of my genitalia, not love. And that was the most painful thing to bear. To think, if I had not gone ahead with the surgery, we would still be together now! But that would have served him, and I would continue to live a lie. And I would never have been happy.

I gave him Fluff, our cat, as a parting gift as I could see he was in a fragile state. I was stronger and while I previously saw a life together with marriage and children, ultimately it did not work out that way. We needed to go our separate ways. If I saw Danny now, I would gasp in fear because I hurt him. I feel guilty for hurting him. I ended everything.

And it is never my intention to hurt anybody. It is not within my nature. But I did what I had to do for me and that was most important.

20. STEPPING OUT

F rom my many past experiences, I knew I was going through a difficult period. Nearly every man I dated since splitting up with my ex, were men with fetishes about transvestites. In the past, it was fine if that was their thing. But I did not want to be someone's fetish, I wanted to be seen and loved as myself, a woman.

Since becoming a woman, I felt much more vulnerable than I previously had a male. I found men's attitude towards women to be oppressive and domineering. They do not always treat women with the respect we deserve. Having experienced both male and female cultures, I became more acutely aware of this trait. Some men are lovely and treat women equally, but they are few and far between!

I have had different experiences. If I tell a man I am transgender, often they will not believe me. And if I do not tell them, I could get hurt if they eventually found out.

If I tell them I am transgender, they may see me as a sexual object rather than Samantha. They might see me as being different.

It is never easy being single. I needed to be selective in my choice of men and trust my instincts when telling someone about my journey.

I started an Instagram (IG) page for education, and it was, at times, quite glamorous. I gained a lot of followers simply by being honest and posting photos about general things. My profile (harveypearsall) was open so anybody could see it. While I knew the risks associated with that, I did not post any personal details and kept the content under tight control.

I discussed my surgery experience there too. I shared on Instagram why I wanted the surgery. It was a good way of giving back and helping others who might find themselves in the same situation as me.

It was never about gaining followers or increasing the number of post likes. It was instead a tool to keep my audience informed and engaged. I know now that many people saw my profile but remained hidden. They were 'lurkers' in that they didn't press 'Like' or comment but seemed to enjoy the content. I was not bothered about Likes, but from a celebrity point of view, someone is always watching. So, you have to know what are they liking and commenting on?

Someone messaged me in my IG Inbox, and we went forward from there. After messaging for a while on IG, we moved to Snapchat, as it did not involve exchanging phone numbers. Then finally we moved to WhatsApp.

The first thing we had to do was scan the QR codes from each other's phones which then encrypted our conversation end-to-end. That greatly reduced the chances of someone ever hacking it.

That would soon become very important as my new life as a single woman would take a very different turn.

21. MEDIA GONE WILD

The biggest issue I faced, was dating ordinary men who had never come across a transgender woman. I met a man who is well known in the media. We exchanged phone number & social media usernames. One night he asked if I would visit his hotel room over in Nantwich, Cheshire.

So, one cold, gloomy night, I drove on the M56 motorway to the A560 and headed down a small, lightly travelled country road which was very wet and dull. I arrived at the Rookery's Hall Hotel, extremely nervous and without any signal on my mobile phone. I placed the phone on dashboard hoping to recover a signal. When one bar appeared, I texted him to say I had safely arrived. He was happy to hear that and said his room number was 403. I walked into the hotel, passed the receptionist with confidence, got on the elevator, and stepped out on the 4th floor. I turned left then right walking along the exceptionally long corridor trying to find number 403. I knocked on the door. I was very nervous life!

No reply?

I knocked again.

No reply.

This is when I sensed there something was not quite right. There was no signal on my phone when I was in the hotel?

Somehow, I manage to connect to the hotel's wi-fi by adding in my details. Once the wi-fi connected a message popped up telling me to return to my car. His boss was shortly visiting his room. I naturally felt very apprehensive, as if I had done something criminal. I walked back, this time taking the stairs. I passed the cleaner and exited a door different to main reception. I saw my car in the car park and walked towards it texting him saying, I can't do this. As I was waited in the car, I saw two couples eating near the bay window.

He replied and reassured me everything was going to be OK and understood why I was nervous. His message somehow put me at ease. Another text came asking if I was still in the car park? His boss had left, and I could return.

I walked back in using the same obscure door from which I exited earlier. I went up and knocked on his door. He opened it.

It all felt a bit surreal as if it was all a dream. He asked if I want a drink. A cup of tea please, I replied (this is my favourite drink). He made me a cuppa and as we sat on the bed, I was noticeably quiet and nervous.

He started talking to me with basic hand gestures. I tried to lipread what he was trying to ask me. Luckily, with my hearing aids and his gestures, I managed to understand what was being said and communicated back.

"Why did you decide to transition," he asked.

I explained I needed to be happy with my true self. He understood that.

He then asked why my skins was so soft, so glowing?

I explained about the hormones tablets I took and how they worked.

He found it all very fascinating.

I was still extremely nervous. The more we talked, the more he made me laugh, and I felt relaxed. He also taught me some of his dance moves in the room and I followed... of course!

His phone had a text message come through. A friend asked if he could pop into our room.

Naturally, he was panicked. I reassured him and said, "I can hide in the bathroom, I'll be OK."

He resisted that idea and instead nipped down to their room for a while. He pretended to be tired and returned to his room. He offered a lot of reassurance which was lovely. We continued to talk, and I taught him some basic sign language such as his name.

He eventually asked if we could watch TV, I said, "yes, please I'd love to watch I'm a Celebrity, Get Me Out of Here." We did and snuggled under the duvet and enjoyed the programme. I will leave the rest to the reader's imagination.

The media have too powerful a hold over famous people's lives. While some deliberately invite scrutiny and coverage, others just want to live life outside the spotlight when not onstage.

If it were not for his fame, he would be able to live a much happier life without being influenced by them. I started to develop feelings for him, but it was clear from the start it could never be more than it was. He was terrified his career could be sabotaged. The media mostly portray trans women as prostitutes. It could not be further from the case. I respected his wishes.

We met over a 2-year period now and then, when we could. He made the boundaries clear right from the start so I knew it would never be more than this, nor did I want it to be.

Also, I think because I am a trans woman, the situation was completely different. We both agreed it would be too much trouble for him if people found out. I've preferred a reserved, quiet life. I didn't want the chaos of media involvement. That fear always lived in the back of my mind. I have this vision of wanting to live a simple, ordinary life. Deep down I knew I couldn't have that with him. That it was not possible.

It was not worth taking the risk and stepping fully into that world. Things may have been different if I wasn't born transgender. The media always portray trans women as prostitutes.

I also did not want to upset my parents. It's not fair for them, just like it's not fair for me. Staying friends with benefits was enough for me. I did not see it as a problem.

That constant fear of what the public will say and think. I neither wanted nor needed that amount of drama.

Prior to meeting him, excitement ruled. And the more I got to know him and saw how things work in his world and how much media and fear of it took over, I had time to really think about what I wanted here. The more I thought about it, the more I knew I just wanted a normal relationship.

The excitement was good at first, but it fizzled out as I/we got used to it. It's not in my nature to upset anyone. It was out of my control. I did not want to sabotage his career and bring negative attention onto him or his family, nor mine.

I knew I deserved better. I met him so many times because we got on so well.

Yes, I met up with other celebrities. I was part of a highly secretive world. I felt safer with him though because he is less well known than the others. The others I would message and meet up once with for a bit of excitement, but because they were more well-known, I didn't pursue it further. Too, I felt more at risk of exposure with them, so I didn't meet up with anyone else multiple times. I cannot classify it as 'dating' since we were never able to go out for a meal or go to the cinema. We were always in a locked room, hidden from the world.

The final straw happened when I told my parents I was going to my friend's house, which was not true. My dad texted Rusty to ask if I was with him and he said 'no, why?' My dad texted back 'Samantha said she was on her way to see you.'

Rusty said 'Samantha is not here with us.' And my mam, the chronic worrier, immediately thought the worst. What if Samantha had an accident? My parents kerb crawled, around the town, trying to find me.

I was in somebody's house having a great time and did not check my phone. And, as an adult, I didn't feel the need to. I have always been secretive. But my parents couldn't find me, Rusty drove around looking for me too. He returned home and told my dad he couldn't find me. When I finally checked my phone, lots of messages came through. My dad phoned the police! That was too much!

My parents worried about me; I understand. Any parent would worry about their child. Remember the incident under the tunnel at age 16? It was a very scary experience for me, but with the risk of it happening again, I thought, it's just not worth it.

My parents always thought I was an angel. Bless them. I was annoyed but they did me a favour. Parents are mostly right, and I was mischievous compared to my 2 brothers. I was no angel. I did realise there's nothing I can hide from my parents. It's impossible. They always find out in the end.

I also give it away too easily with my facial expressions. I cannot keep my face straight. This was also a warning sign telling me this 'relationship' was not worth the risks. Enough was enough.

I felt like I'd been there, done that, got the t-shirt. Is this what I want from life? No.

I want to meet somebody and settle down. That's my aim, and that was the last time I had a relationship like that. I am not that!

I think maybe because I was in a relationship for 6 years I both enjoyed the freedom and excitement of something new and different. Also, as an independent woman, I had some wild oats to sow!

It felt good to have a mutual trust, they know I will never tell a soul. Indeed, the only person who knew is Rusty. He had to know who I was with and where I was going, for my own safety.

I would meet them on weekends. It would just be the 2 of us, which was nice. I would leave my place around 11pm and return around 3 or 4 am, while everyone was sleeping and before sunrise.

If I slept there it was only for a few hours. I wore ultra-trendy clothes... skinny jeans, heels, and a nice top. I would have my hair styled in a blow dry and curls. I enjoyed doing that regularly. I was proud of my long blonde balayage locks. And I loved being pampered. I was just being myself. I did not want to try too hard. If they did not like what they saw, I would not have been bothered. I was not there to please them.

We would drink mostly champagne, and order takeaways from a range of places. We'd watch tv and do other things which, again, I leave to your imagination. We also talked about all sorts of things. I would ask about their lives, nothing too personal but there were some things I wanted to know.

They would ask me about my life, fascinated by how I got to where I am now. They nicknamed me 'A rare breed!' There was something about me. It did not feel like a fetish, they saw me as a woman.

Frankly, I wished all other men thought the same way. We did not argue. The only thing we might have disagreed about was what TV programme to watch! Of course, we always watched TV with subtitles on. This was a new experience for them and most had no idea how to set it up. It was nice to also be seen as a technical expert, I would say to them, 'pass me the remote and I'll do it!'

I felt respected and extremely safe, which was nice. They never did anything that made me feel uncomfortable, nor did they ask me to. They were gentlemen. I was surprised how down to earth these famous people were. I never saw any big egos. They were ordinary people like you and me.

Conversation though had to be much slower. I tried to lipread but sometimes we had a few miscommunications which made us laugh and broke the ice. I tend to be blunt, so my reaction would be 'WHAT?!' We sometimes resorted to writing each other texts on our phones to understand the odd word or two, if we really struggled.

I enjoyed the fun, because it was a completely new experience, different to anything I ever had in my life.

It fizzled out and we are no longer in touch. It was probably all for the best. We knew our limitations and I was able to let it go with the enjoyment of the experience I had. It would be nice if the Government put some measures in place for them to be able to live their lives in privacy and freedom.

Looking back, I regret it as I know I am better and deserved more than that. Life is a learning curve and I went through a phase. As I got older, I became more alert and sensible. I made sure to protect myself.

I want to be a woman who is a good role model. Everybody learns best from their mistakes. I got to a place where I started to think, people can think what they like, they are not angels either!

Life is for exploring. It is a journey. That's how you get to your final destination. Not being accepted for who I am, hurt me deeply.

PART FIVE

FINISHING THE HAT

And when the woman that you wanted goes
You can say to yourself, "Well, I give what I give"
But the women who won't wait for you knows
That, however you live
There's a part of you always standing by
Mapping out the sky, finishing a hat
Starting on a hat, finishing a hat
Look, I made a hat
Where there never was a hat.

FINISHING THE HAT

FROM THE MUSICAL "SUNDAY IN THE PARK WITH GEORGE"

Based on the painting: A Sunday Afternoon on the
Island of La Grande Jatte by Georges Seurat
Written by Stephen Sondheim, 1984

22. LISTEN UP MEN!

eing transgender, my journey is not my only 'men' issue, it is also their perception and lack of education. When I meet straight men, (I am not at all interested in gay men) they react with shock when I tell them I am transgender and instantly volunteer, "I'm not gay."

The issues surrounding my life are the built-in prejudices against trans women. Too, there is an inherent danger in some dating situations. This is an even bigger issue going forward.

Part of why I wrote this book is because more education is needed to understand that *Sexuality and Gender are two completely different things*. Most men need to understand that dating a transgender woman does not change their sexuality. Society does us no favours either. Dating a transgender woman does not make you any less of a man or any less straight. Many men find this difficult to cope with naturally. They often have friends and/or family that are not well educated in matters of sexuality or gender.

This links to the impact of society and being from a different social class as part of an individual's familial upbringing. Some families accept the idea when a member of their family is part of the LGBT community, acceptance is more naturally there. Families that do not have an LGBT member, have greater social class difficulties meeting them. This could come from the stone age or simply a failure to keep up with evolution and acceptance today. Some family do not celebrate diversity in any way. This could be due to peer pressure, coming from an economically or socially deprived hometown, poor education, or just plain ignorance.

Therefore, I always want to be the one responsible for sharing my experience with another. I want to see a larger majority of men become more educated and open-minded about the issues we face in the transgender community.

I just want to be accepted for who I am. This is true for every trans woman. As mentioned earlier, until recently, I realised the first thing I would say if I was approached by a man was, "I am trans." I was always scared of what would happen if they found this out later. But as time went on, I realised being trans does not define someone. I have recently been open about this speaking out in two news articles. for iNews and the Manchester Evening News. I do this to raise awareness and reduce stigma across the transgender community.

The fear of rejection for transgender women is often so real and can be so very hurtful. The majority of trans women just want to feel accepted for who they are. This is why the dating game is so exceedingly difficult for many trans women. Many men say they accept transgender woman right from the start because they claim to be open about it. But, as soon things get too deep and/or the man got what they wanted, they tend to change their mind, using the excuse, "it just didn't work out for us." This is when we trans woman feel most rejected.

A majority of the trans community go through enduring battles of wanting to be accepted and seek approval. Therefore, mental health & depression among members of the trans community can be extensive. Battling through prejudice and the need to justify and explain why a person from the opposite sex should not have to question their sexuality when dating a trans person is incredibly frustrating and depressing.

Being a Deaf, post-operative transgender creates a struggle sometimes when dating someone. Those I tend to date cannot be bothered with the number of issues I face. This left me with a dilemma. Do I open up to a man about my situation right from the start of the relationship? My reasoning is to save my and their time before things get too deeply involved. Or should I just not say anything about my gender identity? Should I instead wait for the right moment when I feel I can open to this person, build their trust? But then the situation has already gotten too deep which eventually means this person could reject me which then leads me to going through more heartache. It is a vicious circle.

This is why I am sharing this experience with everyone, to let everyone who has faced this know, they are never alone!

Sometimes during heartbreak, you just want to say, 'enough is enough.' This pain is too much to bear. That heartbreak made me do things I should not have done.

But I then remind myself every day, someone out there one day will come. It is all about being able to speak openly with family and friends, rather than holding all the pain inside.

Learn to accept it is OK not to be OK. It just is. And feel the courage to talk about it.

I always remind myself I have access to deaf counselling if I feel I will benefit from it. I also seek help by reaching out to those closest to my heart, like Rusty and my Mam and Dad.

A lack of acceptance from friends, family, employers, and a majority of trans people is probably why the suicide rate amongst the transgender community is so high. When we are rejected by those central in our life and society, this naturally makes many trans persons feel isolated and worthless which is a heart-breaking thing to see.

I just want a man to love me, for me.

23. MY LOVING DEAF SUPPORT COMMUNITY

The deaf community is very close-knit. Everyone tends to know each other. I am known within the deaf community, nationally and internationally because of my transgender story. There are few positive role model deaf, post-operative transgender people worldwide. In the UK, very few people have been through the complete reassignment process. I have learned to become 'thick-skinned' which has helped me.

I met this guy who I sort of knew through friends of friends. One night, he spontaneously messaged me through social media. We started to get to know each other better and messaged each other for a few months. We agreed to meet up on a date, and things went very well for few more months. We bounced ideas off each other and there was a good connection. However, it seemed someone else had his heart and that he really did not know what he wanted. This left me with a dilemma.

While devastated by this, I decided my time was precious and called it a day. A few months down the line, he contacted me again and tried to worm his way back into my life. He begged for another chance, even though he already had more than enough chances.

This is where I started to question my own values. I know I deserved better. I know I am a good person. I just never really understood or got an answer as to why I have been treated this way for so long. Was it because I was both transgender and deaf?

The only other Deaf trans person I knew was Mischa, introduced by a mutual friend Laura. Mischa became like a sister to me. We went through the same surgical experience and supported each other. It brought us closer together because we empathised with one another. We often felt like the only Deaf trans people in the world. It was lonely and we knew there had to be many more Deaf trans people out there!

I decided to set up the Facebook DeafTransDivaWorld Group to search for others like us with shared life experiences. It started September of 2014. I was hoping to find similar people. I invited Deaf drag performance artists to the group and hoped they would, in turn, have connections with more people. I saw the numbers multiply. As group Administrator, I would check to see who they were and what their purpose was for joining.

Trans people started to join from Asia, America, Canada, Europe, and Australia. It gave me goose bumps to know there were others out there like me and, at some level, I felt like I was rescuing them. I explained the aim of the group was to work together with people from all over the world, share experiences, and become a strong foundational source for each other and new people.

The group became a mixture of trans drag artists, families of people who are transitioning, and even people looking for love. The group went through periods of heavy traffic and quiet. I posted a video using international sign language to ensure we could all communicate in one language worldwide. Hearing people can't do that Deaf power!

Anyone can post videos to the group and know they're not alone there is a network of people who can support them by commenting on their posts or posting videos back.

In terms of Equality Laws, I knew many other countries were disadvantaged compared to the UK. I had this fire inside of me to want other countries to change, but it wasn't something I could do alone.

I used my influence in the group to become a positive role model and explained why this page is here: for the group to share knowledge and learn from each other. In the UK we are fortunate to have Deaf counselling services. Others may not have that service or support so in our group we become unqualified counsellors in a way drawing on our own experiences to support each other. Nothing can beat first-hand experience when it comes to empathy. It's about empowering others and giving them the courage to fight for change.

I took to Facebook's DeafTransDivaWorld Group in 2014 and posted this:

I have been through a lot in the last 11 years but I have to say it has gone quickly...even thought I have had lots of ups and downs, would I go through all of this journey again?...Yes because I've learnt a lot along the way and it made me become the resilient and assertive person I am today . If you know yourself that you are not happy about your true self, then do something about it.

I do think the NHS should give people more support in this area. But it is perceived that this type of surgery is just cosmetic. But for me I do not feel that is the case. Some Transgender people go through recurring periods of depression because they are not engaged with friends, family, and society in general. They have struggled and at times must do things on their own without support which can often lead to counselling and taking medication for depression, because of their appearance. It can have a long-term effect on their mental health.

In the end the NHS will end up paying more to the transgender person, for other treatment than maybe it would have cost for surgery in the first place. I strongly believe that the NHS should fund some part of hair transplants, laser treatment to cover the full cost for facial hair removal, as they have an 8-session limit, but not necessarily provide funding for breast augmentation. They do however fund the gender reassignment surgery.

I think the NHS should fund some toward hair transplants, as appearance is especially important to the transgender person as most people base their opinion on first impressions, but this is just my opinion.

I turned 30 and a truly diverse group of friends attended my party. To see so many diverse members of my community together, really opened my parent's eyes.

I decided to travel to Marbella for my birthday and had the time of my life. I also travelled that milestone year to Los Angeles & Las Vegas on a long around-the-world road trip ending down under in Sydney, Australia.

I met a guy from Northern Ireland, and we had an initial whirlwind romance. I honestly thought he could be 'the one.' I was getting lots of love, attention, beautiful gifts such as Christian Louboutin heels, and a French bulldog as a Valentine's Day gift. It was all a big, lovely surprise. I flew over to visit him in Northern Ireland on a regular basis.

Sadly, with no reason given, he went to Australia over Christmas and New Year's. I later learned it was to care for his ill father. This was understandable. Once again though, I hardly heard anything from him. Despite numerous texts and emails. all I got were feeble excuses. "I'm really busy here taking care of my dad and will be home within next few weeks..." It was now 6-months later. That is when he ghosted me, and our relationship ended. This was his loss but also my gain.

24. FINISHING THE HAT

I had grown so much since my surgery. I loved returning to Marbella because I felt relaxed there. It was becoming my second home. The stress is left far behind whenever I arrive at Puerto Banus. It's the most beautiful town and it's not a long flight from Manchester. So, it's easy to escape to the sun, and it became a perfect holiday destination for me.

Since ending the relationship with Danny, I now had some money to spend on myself. The new car bug bit me hard and I wanted a new one. This time, having learned my lesson, I spoke to Rusty, and he suggested we go around and have a look at which car I might like. He advised me to not buy a new car. Because I tend to buy things in the spur of the moment. I am known for taking rash decisions. However, on the return trip home, he knew instantly what I was up to, it's impossible for me to hide my emotions from my best friend. So, I grinned and said, "I just bought my first ever top of the line Mercedes Benz GLA."

As soon I received my new car, I was over the moon with it. And a few weeks further down the line, I realised I'd made the wrong decision. I really needed to buy my first home. Sacrifice was a lesson I still had to learn. I decided the car was the one thing I had to get rid of.

With help from my parents, I eventually bought my first ever home, in the most desirable place. It was a smart decision to get rid of my black Mercedes. I could not have both for the time being.

As my maturity continues now as a woman, I began to look to the future of helping others. I would love to be able to set up workshops that teach transgender identity in schools and colleges. They would be professional workshops that raise awareness of transgender issues, especially within deaf community.

I would also love to be able to set up Deaf transgender workshop from the Facebook group I established. I spoke with every member via Facebook video message. I would love to be able to invite every one of them to the UK for this transgender workshop where we would communicate in one language (International Sign Language) to exchange our wealth of personal experiences. This has proven exceedingly difficult due to a lack of funding and resources.

MY DREAMS:
To narrate and convert this book into a British Sign Language/International Sign Language video or see it made into a film for the theatrical release to raise awareness and empower the deaf transgender community worldwide.

I want them to know that they are not alone. Why share my story in-depth? I feel if I don't share my experiences then issues of discrimination and exclusion will continue forever. Instead of hiding behind taboos and stigmas, the lack of education was very difficult. I am very fortunate to be resilient.

Now, in 21st Century, laws are changing everywhere allowing us to live our lives to the fullest without fear or shame.

I hope my story becomes a role model that empowers other. There is no better legacy for Deaf transgender individuals than to look up to someone who has walked this long journey to freedom. It gives me great satisfaction to help them realise they are not alone and can live their life free from rejection or oppression.

While reading this book, you may have noticed several times I said, 'it all goes back to education'. While I know this can be controversial, as a trans woman who is deaf, I bring a unique perspective. So many global issues produce rigidly divided reactions. While everyone is entitled to their own opinion, they are entitled to their own set of facts.

My goal is help bring an open-minded perspective, take individual beliefs into account and respect that as I hope to raise their consciousness around this issue and treat deaf trans people with respect.

It is down to upbringing and culture creating an unconscious bias which affects their perceptions, media, educational, and political influences. This is what creates division in this world.

When I say, 'it goes back to education,' governments and our leaders need to investigate systemic flaws, to see where everything went so wrong. Parents are taught, 'it's just a phase.' And that approach creates so much damage for the child.

From a medical perspective, they may mean well but it does little good for either the child or the parents. It creates numerous mental health problems, fear, and anxiety.

Society hugely influences the child and their parents, which in turn assigns right and wrong when children should not be made to feel abnormal when it comes to THEIR gender expression.

Fear of 'coming out' should not exist. When children are born, they are assumed to be straight and their birth assigned gender. Where does that come from? If not straight, they have the added pressure and fear of feeling different. Imagine having to tell people that they don't fit into that category?

They should not have to feel like this.

Before babies are born, their gender can be revealed. Assumptions are made, 'it's a boy!' And then the extension thinking becomes, I wonder what he will do when he's older? What will his future wife be like? I can't wait to have grandchildren...

Newsflash parents. While you have a huge influence in your child's life, it's not about you! You have one job, give your children roots and wings. You want them to grow up and become who they feel they really are. You give them the best you can in love, education, and morality. And at the end of the day?

It's not about you. Your children need that strong imprinting and upbringing and more than anything they need you to listen to and not dismiss them when they say, "I think I am different from who you think I am...

I advocate for people to be open-minded, when you have a baby boy, yes be excited, of course, but also consider that this child may want to identify with the LGBTQIA+ community.

You may have perceptions about what your child is going to be like but allow them to express themselves for who they truly are and want to become. Every individual has the right to be able to express their true selves and be happy.

And this is where the wings come in. When they are ready to take on their own lives in their own way, you must let go and... let them be themselves. Let them fly from the nest. Pick them up if they fall, nurse them back to health and let them go again!

What we teach in schools needs to be broader. Instead of just focusing on the biology of sex education, man plus woman equals baby. There is more to the story! People today have children through different means. Sime families have parent(s) within the LGBTQIA+ community. Teaching children about the acceptability of this, reduces their likelihood of being bullied.

Children should be taught that difference and diversity are beautiful things. Regardless of age, ability, gender, ethnicity, religious belief, culture, size, etc. Everyone is individual and different and that is what makes the world a beautiful place to live. The variety.

Long term outcomes would be so much better and there was less division in this world if people were taught to love each other regardless of their background. It's not rocket science to respect each other!

The readers of this book can see the journey I went through even with parental support and the rights I have as a citizen of this country - imagine what it's like for others in third world countries where it is illegal in some cases. The struggle must be so traumatic, and their mental state must be so fragile naturally I wanted to support as much as I can. I know I can't support every single person directly, but I have made a difference.

It's within my nature to show love. I had so much love from my parents and I wanted to give my love to those who went through the same experience. I know some don't have family experiences like I did so I felt a bit guilty in a way. I know I was privileged in that respect, but I didn't want that to allow me to ignore what's happening out there.

Being ignorant is not an attractive way to be it's all about humanity. The numbers are booming and at the time of writing there are 814 members. The group will always be carefully managed because of the risks associated with it there are 5 admins who will try our best to make sure that it's a safe space with genuine people. It is our dream to be able to meet up, but it has not been possible. There are visa limitations people having passports in a different gender to their identity financial difficulties communication barriers.

I would love to see the Deaf trans group to become a charity one day and to help those who need it globally. It will be a long process with extreme difficulty, but we'll get there. Again, I know I won't be able to do this alone, it's not possible. My dream is to see everybody in the same room it will probably be my biggest achievement in my lifetime. LGBTQIA+ organisations can work in partnerships as allies but being trans is more complex and needs to have specific support and attention hence the reason for setting up a separate group. It makes me so happy to see trans people blossoming I feel like I am watering them with positivity.

Too, our country's leaders need to look at their own cabinets. They have always been male dominated and lacked diversity. For those without members of the LGBTQIA+ community a question. How are they supposed to feel represented when it comes to decision making and policy? Some cabinets have members of the LGBTQIA+ community. However, many have only 'come out' after being appointed and that is sad to see. Do they feel that they wouldn't have been successful if they had come out beforehand?

Historically, there's not been a transgender MP appointed to the UK cabinet. My argument is, how can the government decide on transgender issues? While they may consult with experts, it's not the same.

We are supposed to be a multicultural country but that's not the case. I strongly feel each culture and minority should be represented in the cabinet, to meet a quota. The law in the UK states that businesses must comply with the Equality Act. However, they are not leading by example when it comes to those who are in the Cabinet.

Organisations and people across the UK are becoming more forward thinking about diversity, While the public is headed in the right direction, it feels like the UK and US Governments are going backwards. Some policies and laws are being reversed and that creates division. They should instead work on improving existing policies to see what can be done better, rather than reverse the work and progress that has already been done because of ideological or evangelical purposes!

If we all just found a way to accept each other's differences and became allies, the world would be a much more beautiful place to live.

AFTERWORD - TOMORROW

*E*verything in this book is my opinion. And it is borne out through a lifetime of actual experience. Imagine being stuck for two decades of your life in the wrong body, being finally freed, and then having to face so many obstacles to finding relationship happiness ...

My greatest lesson over the years? I am an independent woman who doesn't need a man to support and/or fulfil my dreams. And it would be nice to have someone to go home to who would unconditionally love me for who I am.

The negative encounters I had with so many men affected my self-esteem, confidence, and brought out my insecurities. I tended to think all men were like that and now am sure there is a man out there looking for me and vice versa. I will love to have an ordinary life just like everyone else's. A place of our own that we call home, children of our own, and getting married! That's not much to ask, is it?

Money is not the answer, but let's be real, it helps to certain extent. The two most important things in life for me is to have someone love me and then accept me as Samantha, not Richard.

When time is right, I would love to start my own family, whether or not I have a future partner. I am determined to build a family of my own and would look at either adoption, surrogate mother, or womb transplant (which is becoming a thing.) Not sure if this has been successful yet as more research is needed.

All I have ever wanted is for someone to love me for me and treat me like the desired and desirable woman I am, without the burden of any label.

And a benefit of finishing THIS 'hat' and publishing this book, was meeting a new partner. Could it be THE ONE? Well, that is another chapter for this ongoing story.

Look, I made a hat

Where there never was a hat!

ACKNOWLEDGMENTS

T hanks to my mam and dad who have supported me through thick and thin. My rocks forever and always! X

Thanks to my two brothers who have put up with me and are still very supportive!

Thanks to my wider family who have always loved me, cared for me and despite it not being easy for them or me, but who welcomed me as Samantha with open arms. I cannot thank you enough.

Thanks to my best friend Rusty, who has always been there for me. I'm unsure of where you get your patience from, but I know that no matter what, you'll always be there for me! You are definitely irreplaceable.

Thanks to my wider circle of friends who have accepted me for who I am and continue to be there for me when I need them most.

Thanks to my sister from another mister – Mischa. We were the only trans females in the Deaf community at that time and can both totally relate to each other. We shared the same experience and could empathise with each other at a time when nobody else could. Love you endlessly.

Thank you to my previous and current employers, who have accepted me for who I am and been very supportive during my transition and still are to this day. Cannot thank you enough!

My thanks to Charing Cross Hospital in Hammersmith London, where I underwent my gender reassignment surgery. Cannot thank you enough for doing such an amazing job and you are the people who transformed my life! The NHS can at times be taken for granted, but in my situation you did an amazing job and I want this to be recognised.

Website: https://tavistockandportman.nhs.uk/

A special thanks to Paige Louise and the rest of the team for taking the time to teach me how to apply make up. On a few occasions you managed to 'fit me in' despite being fully booked. You always made me feel welcomed and I cannot thank you enough as ever since my make up style has vastly improved.

Website: https://www.plouise.co.uk/

A special thanks to my hair transplant surgeon - Dr Farjo - who has transformed my image. Prior to meeting you I thought there would be no cure to my receding hairline and I was depressed as a result; you removed this depression overnight, that's how quick the results were.

Website: https://www.farjo.com/

A special thanks to Dr Professor Gerard Byrne at Spire Hospital - Oncoplastic breast surgeon - who carried out my breast enlargement surgery which boosted my confidence.

Website: https://www.spirehealthcare.com

Dr Aslani and Dr Bravo from the Cirumed Clinic in Marbella who carried out my Brazilian butt lift surgery with fat transfer. One of the key experiences for me as it transformed by physical shape into one of an hour-glass. You did an amazing job!

Website: https://cirumed.es/english/

Thanks to the Dental Centre Turkey for my full set of dental crowns. I haven't stopped smiling since.

Website: https://dentalcentreantalya.com/

And thank you to you, the reader, for taking the time to read this book through to the end. It means a lot to me.

**One final thanks to everyone listed above,
you have all enabled me to blossom
into the person who I am today.**

TO LEARN MORE:

This journey would not be possible without the many support organisations who helped me to become the woman I am today. I list them here, how to contact and where you can find, follow, and contact me.

DeafTrans/DivaWorld - https://www.facebook.com/groups/DeafTrans-DivaWorld

Deaf Transgender Awareness Workshop - https://www.facebook.com/groups/243487116658414

Deaf LGBTIQA- http://deaflgbtiqa.org.uk/

Instagram - Harveypearsall

Twitter - SamanthaPearsa1

Contact me: Deaftransworkshop@gmail.com

PHOTO GALLERY

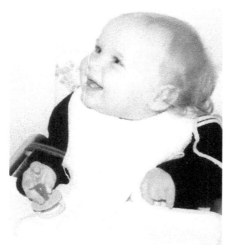

I was a happy baby boy. While I was not in the hearing world, I felt the overwhelming love of my family.

My childhood home. Note the large picture window from which I sat and watched the world go by.

Me as a baby in my parents' bed with my older brothers Phillip (C) and Matthew (R)

My mother, my rock, always adored me as Richard and later as Samantha.

My Dad and my Gran also loved me very much as a little boy.

My older brothers took special care of their younger brother.

My primary school picture from age 6 or 7 (1993-1994)

My football trophy for team MVP for 200-'07 was presented by Steve McLaren, professional football manager for the England National team and most recently Manager of Queens Park Rangers (QPR).

As I grew older and became a teenage boy, I became unhappier with the changes in my body. This was a very difficult time for me.

The boy in the middle of this photo pre-surgery was ME! Here I am with mamand dad, Matthew and his girlfriend, now wife...

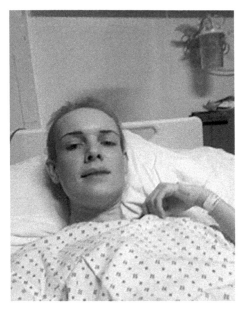

The night before my re-assignment surgery. My last night as Richard.

My first day post-op following the hair transplant surgery.

After my hair translplant, I was helped by a top make-up artist, Paige Louise who taught me everything I needed to know!

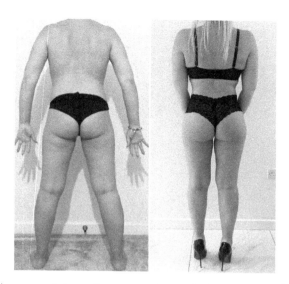

One of the more interesting procedures during my transformation was a cosmetic procedure done at the Cirumed Clinic in Marbella, Spain. The Brazilian 'butt tuck' turned my male derriere into a more proportioned female looking one. The doctor transferred fat from my stomach into the back of my buttocks to enhance its curve.

Marbella became a second home for me. A short flight from Manchester, it had many things home did not, mostly beaches, calm and sun... lots of sun!

My bestie Rusty and I enjoyed Turkey together where he was my nursemaid dring my teeth surgery and we both loved clubbing back home in Manchester!

As a free woman, I spent a lot of time travelling post-surgery enjoying US Route 66, The Grand Canyon and Las Vegas!

The real rock stars in my life are my wonderful parents. My Dad rescued me more times than one could ever imagine and my Mom was always there and grieved the loss of her son Richard. And both came to know and deeply love me as Samantha. This was them at my huge 30th birthday celebration in 2017

It was an epic party for the ages and a great celebration
of my new womanhood and freedom!

With my gal pals at a massive Spice girls concert in
Edinburgh. Manchester was sold-out but we loved the Spicve
Girls so much, we were ready and willing to travel!

This is the glamourous woman I am today. It was
a long journey and worth every moment.

Lightning Source UK Ltd.
Milton Keynes UK
UKHW021146040821
388300UK00013B/570